THE SCALPEL
AND THE CROSS

Also by Gene L. Green

The Majority World Theology Series
(ed. Gene L. Green, K. K. Yeo, Stephen T. Pardue)

Global Theology in Evangelical Perspective:
Exploring the Contextual Nature of Theology and Mission
(ed. Gene L. Green, Jeffrey P. Greenman)

The New Testament in Antiquity
(with Gary M. Burge and Lynn H. Cohick)

Jude and 2 Peter
(Baker Exegetical Commentary on the New Testament)

The Letters to the Thessalonians
(Pillar New Testament Commentary)

1 y 2 Tesalonicenses

1 Pedro y 2 Pedro
(Comentario Biblico Hispanoamericano)

ORDINARY THEOLOGY SERIES

THE SCALPEL AND THE CROSS

A THEOLOGY OF
SURGERY

GENE L. GREEN

ZONDERVAN®

ZONDERVAN

The Scalpel and the Cross
Copyright © 2014 by Gene L. Green

This title is also available as a Zondervan ebook. Visit www.zondervan.com/ebooks.

Requests for information should be addressed to:
Zondervan, 3900 *Sparks Dr. SE, Grand Rapids, Michigan 49546*

Library of Congress Cataloging-in-Publication Data

Green, Gene L., author.
    The scalpel and the cross : a theology of surgery / Gene L. Green.
      pages cm
    ISBN 978-0-310-51605-7
    1. Medicine–Religious aspects–Christianity. 2. Surgery–Miscellanea.
  I. Title.
  BT732.2.G74   2014
  261.5'61–dc23   2014018869

Cover design: Mikah Kandros
Interior illustration: Beth Shagene
Interior design: Beth Shagene

Printed in the United States of America

15 16 17 18 19 20 /DCI/ 21 20 19 18 17 16 15 14 13 12 11 10 9 8 7 6 5 4 3 2 1

Medicis carissimis

James Carroll, M.D.
Robin Fortman, A.P.N., C.N.P
George Kuzycz, M.D.
Mark Nelson, M.D.

CONTENTS

FOREWORD TO THE ORDINARY THEOLOGY SERIES

Gene L. Green

ORDINARY THEOLOGY. THESE TWO WORDS TOGETHER SOUND LIKE an oxymoron. We're accustomed to thinking about "theology" as the stiff and stifling stuff found in ponderous tomes written by Christian scholars in ivory towers, places far removed from our ordinary lives. We live on the street, in our homes, in places of business, in schools, in gyms, and in churches. What does theology have to do with the ordinary affairs of our daily lives?

We want to bring the Bible into our lives, to be sure, and we attend church to learn about God's Word. We read our favorite passages and wonder how ancient stories about Noah on the water or Jesus on the water relate to the checkout at the grocery store, the hours at work, the novel we read for pleasure, the sicknesses we endure, the votes we cast, or the bed. How do we construct a bridge between the biblical worlds and the twenty-first-century world as we seek to follow Jesus faithfully? The distance between our local shopping center and Paul's forum in Athens (Acts 17) seems like an unbridgeable canyon. What does the Bible have to do with the wonderful or difficult realities we face on the baseball field or in the city? How do we receive God's Word, which is truly for all people, at all times, in all places?

It's an old question, one the church has been asking for centuries. The Bible is a historical document with contemporary relevance. But we're also aware that it doesn't seem to speak directly to many situations we face. There is no obvious biblical view of nuclear war, a kind of destruction unknown in the ancient world. What about epidemics such as AIDS, an unknown disease in the ancient world? The Noah story describes a dramatic climate change, but does that cataclysm have anything to do with global warming today? Through the centuries, Christians have understood that the Bible cannot be simply proof-texted in all life's situations. Yet we still believe that the Bible is God's word for us in our complex world. Enter theology.

The word *theology* comes from a couple of Greek terms: *theos* and *logos*. *Theos* means "God" and *logos* means "word." Simply stated, theology is words that express thoughts about God. We hold beliefs about God such as "God is love" (1 John 4:8). We understand that Jesus died for our sins and that we have a hope that transcends the grave because of the resurrection of Christ. All these are theological statements. We have received Christian theology through our parents, church, and Scripture reading, and we attempt to find how biblically based belief relates to our lives. We do theology as we take Scripture and our inherited theology and seek to work out what God is saying about the issues of today. Every Christian is a theologian.

Ordinary theology is, really, just another way to say *theology*. The expression emphasizes how theology is part of the ordinary stuff of daily life. Food is a theological topic. We can think about buying food, the need for food, those without food, selling food. What does the Bible have to say about food supply, hunger, and generosity? To ask that question is to think theologically about food. What about government welfare or foreign aid? We can think through the whole of Scripture and apply its perspectives and teachings to such issues. This is theology. And it is something every Christian can and must do. We believe that the gospel is relevant not only to our inner life, but to life in the world. The road we travel as ordinary Christians is to do "ordinary theology" as we work God's message into all aspects of daily life.

The Ordinary Theology Series has a few goals. The first is to take up the common issues of daily life and think through them theologically. But another purpose of the series is to invite you to develop your skills as a theologian. These small books are examples of theological method but also a welcome into the necessary, challenging, and joyous task of doing theology. We're all called to follow the example of the first great Christian theologian whose day job was netting fish for a living. Peter did not receive training in the rabbinic schools as had Paul, yet he was the one who first understood and stated that Jesus was the Christ, the Son of the Living God (Matt. 16:16). He also opened the door of faith to the Gentiles as he came to understand that God accepts every person, regardless of ethnicity (Acts 10). Each of us can make a theological contribution to the church, our family, our community, and our own life. For your sake and the sake of others, be a theologian.

One final word about format. Each chapter begins with a story, and theological reflection follows. Theology happens in the place where Scripture meets us on the road where "life is lived tensely, where thought has its birth in conflict and concern, where choices are made and decisions are carried out."* We go to Scripture and the deep well of Christian theology as we develop our theology in the place where we find ourselves. God is concerned about people and places and does not ask us to divorce ourselves from them as we follow and serve Christ. And he gives us guidance on how to do that. So, enjoy the read! And again: be the theologian.

---

* John MacKay, *A Preface to Christian Theology* (New York: Macmillan, 1941), 27.

INTRODUCTION
(PLEASE READ THIS!)

Y OU'RE NOT GOING TO CHINA," DR. CARROLL ANNOUNCED AFTER reading the results of my hurriedly scheduled echocardiogram. "You're going in for surgery."

For a moment the explosive words left me speechless, yet I clearly understood. During the preceding weeks, while preparing to teach a course on 1 Peter at Peking University, I had felt increasingly exhausted and out of breath when cycling, running on the treadmill, or even trimming hedges. My wife, a medical professional, wisely insisted that I visit my doctor before embarking on the long, strenuous journey to China. Jim Carroll, my cardiologist, explained that my aortic valve was calcified to the point that the blood flow through it had become restricted, accounting for my symptoms. I needed to have the valve replaced and undergo a single coronary bypass graft as well. Surgery was imminent.

The days preceding the surgery were filled with a myriad of housekeeping activities, including paying bills, drawing up a new will "just in case," calling the insurance company to check on coverage, and talking with my wife and daughters about the surgery and our future. We all believed I would come through well, but prudence dictated that we at least look at what life would be like for them should the operation not have a happy outcome. Just as my wife likes leaving the house in order when we head out on vacation, so too I wanted to be able to focus on the surgery and recovery without worrying about my family's well-being. Best leave things tidy.

In the middle of the preparations, however, I realized that surgery was more than a technical medical procedure. A whole history, stretching back to the Greco-Roman era, undergirds the surgical procedure I was about to undergo. The modern operating theater is radically cleaner than it was in the nineteenth-century hospital when Joseph Lister began using antiseptics to reduce infections. He had become aware of the germ theory developed by Louis Pasteur. The contemporary surgeon stands on the shoulders of centuries of medical personnel and practice.

Not only is surgery connected with history, but it also has a social dimension. Surgeons undertake their work in concert with other medical professionals who labor together within the confines of the modern hospital run by administrators and staffed with scores of support personnel.

Surgery intersects economics as well. The cost was going to be exorbitant, I knew, and so I made sure that everything was done within the parameters outlined by my insurance company. Surgery is about more than scalpels and skills.

As a Christian, I also began to ask questions about the relationship between my faith in Christ and what I would soon experience. How does my understanding of the Bible and Christian theology frame what was going to occur in the operating room? To be sure, I wanted people to pray for me — before, during, and after the operation. I trusted God to help the surgeon and help me.

But was surgery part of another story, *God's story*, as expressed in the Bible and brought to bear on the great questions of every age through Christian theology? We know the bedrock themes that uphold the Christian faith: God created the world; humanity fell into sin in rebellion against him; God not only brought judgment upon humanity but offered a promise of redemption as well; that promise began to reach its fulfillment in the incarnation, life, death, resurrection, and ascension of Jesus Christ; we anticipate the full realization of God's promise when Christ returns. His kingdom comes and his will will be done on earth as it is in heaven. Indeed, his coming kingdom has broken into the present as both John the Baptist and Jesus taught us (Matt. 3:1 – 2; 4:17; Luke 17:21, "the kingdom of God is in your midst"). As Christians, we live within these great moments of God's plan for humanity and all of his creation. In other words, our life is part of Christian theology. How we think about what happens in our life, and our reflections about how we should live, are intertwined with God's great deeds and his truth recorded for us in the Bible. Our life and what we do is tied together with God and what he does. For the Christian, life and theology cannot be separated. They are joined at the hip.

We understand this well when we debate some of the critical moral issues of our age. Our affirmation that human life is a gift from God gives us great pause and moves us to action as we consider questions about abortion or euthanasia. Our theological convictions commonly enter into our discussions and actions surrounding these issues. Similarly, during the Civil War, theological questions permeated the debates about abolishing slavery, with different interpretations of the Bible going head-to-head in the midst of the move to secede from the Union and to engage in war.[1] So too, many leaders in the Civil Rights movement found guidance and clarity from Scripture. Likewise, our political discussion at the beginning of the twenty-first century intersects questions that arise from our faith, making some civic discourse extremely theological in nature whether the topic is healthcare or the nature of marriage.

So, if we bring the Bible and theology into our understanding of the nature of humanity and the beginning of life, into questions of human and civil rights, and into our debates about healthcare and marriage, why should we isolate medical care and surgery from our theology? Is it possible to construct a theology of surgery that helps us examine this medical event under the intense light of the

Christian faith? Can theology lead us to informed Christian thinking about how surgery should be carried out? To put it another way, does a Christian perspective on surgery only mean that we should pray for the patient and the surgeon? Does it have a place in God's plan, and can we think about it more holistically, more *theologically*?

This exercise may seem alien to some who are used to keeping medicine and faith, or faith and science, neatly compartmentalized. In the liberal arts college where I teach, however, we are accustomed to thinking with our students about what *A* has to do with *B*. For example, we can bring sociological perspectives to bear on the process language learning and Bible reading. History and art inform each other. "The integration of Faith and learning" becomes a key concern in Christian liberal arts education.[2]

So, at this time of surgery, I invite you to walk along with me as we talk about theology and surgery. Recognizing that God permeates every aspect of our private and public lives is a good place to start this conversation. Is anything autonomous from him? What about the operating room?

Upon reading a draft of this manuscript, my brother asked, "Who are you writing this for?" Good question. In the first instance, I wrote it for myself as I faced major surgery. I didn't have any resources on my bookshelf to help me think through the upcoming procedure in light of my faith. If the truth be known, the prospect of going under the knife made me extremely nervous. I needed to bring my faith into the center of this large and life-altering (or life-ending) event to help me settle down!

But I also wrote it for the many others who are looking ahead to or looking back on their surgical experience. The message I want to whisper in my fellow patients' ears is that there is a deep river of faith that runs through surgery. I would like to offer this short book to surgeons as well, who, together with their patients, are thinking about questions of faith, hope, and meaning as they enter the operating theater. This essay is in part a thanksgiving for their lifesaving work. Hopefully these reflections will benefit ministers of the gospel too, as those who come to counsel and comfort patients, their families, and friends. In the end, I have multiple audiences in mind. My desire is that through this short book many will begin to think in new ways about surgery and Christian theology.

1

REFLECTIONS FROM
THE DAY BEFORE

Tomorrow they cut.*

A few years ago my cardiologist informed me that the echo-cardiogram showed a buildup of calcium on my aortic valve. Some-day the valve would need to be replaced since the blood flow through it would become severely restricted. I had been in the battle against high cholesterol for a couple of decades and enjoyed good success through adjusting my diet, exercise, and modern pharmacology. I imagined that staving off open-heart surgery would be possible as well. Ten, fifteen, or twenty years were the projections I had in mind before the surgeon would need to install a mechanical or bioengi-neered prosthetic in place of my native valve. My calculations were off significantly. A mere two years passed before I found myself short of breath after a short ride on my titanium road bike. Pains in the upper chest forced me to stop for rest. The same pain came when I ran my customary programs on the treadmill. Even trimming the hedges became disconcertingly difficult. This twice-yearly project had never brought much joy, but it never sent me to my seat either, short of breath, at least until now.

I made an appointment with my trusted GP, Mark Nelson. After hearing that I had become symptomatic, he submitted a referral that

---

* The first draft of this chapter was written a day before going in for surgery.

allowed me to make an appointment with my cardiologist, Jim Carroll, and Robin Fortman, my PA (physician's assistant) whose specialization is cardiology. Carroll ordered an angiogram after seeing the results from the echocardiogram Fortman had ordered. Both exams, along with my symptoms, clearly indicated that the time for surgery had come. He also discovered a blocked coronary artery that would need to be bypassed using a vein taken from my leg and grafted onto my heart. Surgery was imminent. The instructions were simple: No food or water after midnight; take morning medications with a sip of water; scrub down thoroughly with antibacterial cloths in the morning; put on freshly cleaned clothes for the trip to the hospital. Tomorrow they cut.

During the days of preparation, I read countless journal articles about aortic valve replacement as part of the decision to opt for a mechanical valve fabricated from carbon or a biological valve donated by a fellow creature. Porcine, bovine, or equine were the options, all of which echoed myths of satyrs, minotaurs, and centaurs. Other techniques are under development such as the Ross procedure, which uses a person's own pulmonary valve in the place of the aortic valve, necessitating the graft of a replacement pulmonary valve harvested from a cadaver. The technology involved to assure good hemodynamics and to maintain structural integrity of the biological valves inspires awe. On the other hand, the fabrication and installation of a small, carbon valve brings science fiction straight into the heart as the procedure transforms a person into a cyborg. I had an embarrassment of technology at my disposal to help assure an extended lifespan. Without the operation I was looking at two to five years of life left. Not good.

But through all the literature I discovered nothing written that could be called a theology of surgery. How should I be thinking about the forthcoming surgery in relation to my faith in Christ, my theology? The medical journals were not the place to look for such reflection, and I did not expect the surgeon to discuss this matter with me. Though I was filled full with good medical understanding about this necessary surgery and had numerous technological questions occupying my mind, there was no theological river running through it.* The prayers of the saints were going up across the world, and I knew God heard them and would answer. God is the Physician and all physicians receive their calling from him. Only he, in the end, can heal. But beyond these basic theological pillars, I had not inherited clear and wise guidance on how to reflect more broadly on the place of surgery within God's plan and purpose. I had no theology of surgery, only a doctor's black bag of technology. Theology shapes our understanding of God, his world, his societies, and ourselves. The theological support for surgery was not there, however. The framing was absent.† Curious, indeed.

In the book *Philosophie de la Chirurgie*, René Leriche observed, "Surgery is an act of human authority on destiny."[3] Surgeons impose their will upon the human body in an attempt to correct that which destiny dictated with the hope that this intervention will help restore the person to better functionality. The surgeon faces off against malformation and deterioration, broken body parts and malignant growths, in a strong man's bid to bring the offending body part under control. Something has gone wrong, and the surgeon musters the best of knowledge, skill, and art to correct it and restore the person. Cutting the body is a violent yet noble business, an imposition of authority upon a destiny that boasts an absolute claim of sovereignty. In this wrestling match, there are victories through the pain, as well as casualties and tears. But despite the way both surgeon and patient may limp away on inglorious days, both reassemble on the line to wrest the outcomes of destiny once again from her hand.‡

The audacity and violence of the surgical act stand up even under Hippocrates' dictum to "never do harm." The surgeon does

---

* This essay does not address questions and perspectives surrounding elective surgery.

† Even Google and the ATLA Religion Index databases yield extremely few and shallow results.

‡ *Moira* was the goddess of destiny in Greek myth.

not administer the controlled violence of the scalpel with harmful intent or destructive force but sharply cuts with care and precision. The surgeon and their patient accept the wounds as part of the price when saying "No!" Restoration, not harm, is the goal of this agonizing engagement.

The act of surgery finds its archetype in the art and skill of Jesus whose healings resembled the surgeon's work more than any other branch of medicine. He imposed his authority on the deformations that surrounded everyone from Galilee to Judea, and he even healed the wounded. When Peter sought to do harm by cutting off the ear of Malchus, the high priest's slave (John 18:10), Luke the Physician notes that Jesus "touched the man's ear and healed him" (Luke 22:51). We do not know whether he picked the whole ear up off the ground or reattached the ear that hung by a piece of flesh from Malchus's head. He acted as a surgeon in either case, divinely suturing the wound without further loss of blood or any malformation. Luke does not stop long enough to let us know if a scar remained. Jesus imposed a higher order on this moment of destiny, both for Malchus and himself, as he was being arrested. Peter acted as someone entangled by the plans laid out by others to do Jesus harm, but Jesus stepped up to take control, commanding Peter to put up his sword and adding, "No more of this!"

Earlier in Jesus' ministry, those gathered around the pool of Bethsaida in Jerusalem saw that Jesus could take authority over deformations in the human body (John 5:2 – 15). The blind, the lame, and the paralyzed all gathered at this pool, which at other times in its history became associated with the Greek god of healing, Asclepius. Myth and superstition surround the scene as people apparently expected healing if they could get into the water when it stirred by some mysterious power (John 5:6 – 7). A man who was lame for thirty-eight years waited by the pool. His case was hopeless. He had never walked and never would walk. But Jesus simply commanded, "Get up! Pick up your mat and walk" and "At once the man was cured." He did as Jesus commanded, picking up his mat and walking. The Surgeon intervened where time and destiny had stamped their mark of defeat. The patient's task was simply to believe and obey the Surgeon's instructions.

Not everyone received healing from Jesus, though there are numerous scenes throughout the gospel records that report the remarkable efficacy of Jesus' work as the Physician (Luke 6:9; 9:11). The news spread and the crowds swelled, even to the point that Jesus could no longer walk openly (Mark 2:4, 13; 3:9, 20; 5:24, 27; 6:34; 7:33). Compassion for the crowds motivated all his actions (Mark 8:2). In Jesus' day physicians were available and Luke, Paul's travel companion, was one of them by training and trade (Col. 4:14). Healing centers such as Epidaurus celebrated the cult of Asclepius, and many who slept in the *abaton* within the precincts of his temple, the Asclepion, sought healing. But no physician was ever as effective and no god ever generated as much acclaim as Jesus, the Healer.

Yet even with great numbers healed, some did not receive his benefaction. A man lame from birth, who lay daily at a busy gate of the Temple in Jerusalem, had seen Jesus walk by on numerous occasions yet he remained lame. Jesus passed on his healing ministry to his disciples. We know that after his resurrection and ascension Peter and John passed by and caught the lame man's gaze. Peter said to him, " 'In the name of Jesus Christ of Nazareth, walk.' Taking him by the right hand, he helped him up, and instantly the man's feet and ankles became strong" (Acts 3:6 – 7). The Great Surgeon acted again through the one he had called and commissioned in this work. Peter acted with faith in the Surgeon and believed fully that a lifetime of destiny could be overruled by Jesus Christ of Nazareth's authority. The surgery was a stellar success since the man went away "walking, and leaping, and praising God." He had recognized an outstretched hand that was not Peter's. But this man for years had seen Jesus walk by and was not touched by him. Jesus healed, but sometimes people did not receive this grace.

When Jesus explained to the disciples of John the Baptist that he was indeed the one who was promised by the prophets, Jesus answered by referring to Isaiah 35, "Go back and report to John what you hear and see: The blind receive sight, the lame walk, those who have leprosy are cleansed, the deaf hear, the dead are raised, and the good news is proclaimed to the poor" (Matt. 11:4 – 5). The words come from one of the chapters in Isaiah that describes Yahweh's victory on behalf of his people:

> Be strong, do not fear;
> your God will come,
>   he will come with vengeance;
> with divine retribution
>   he will come to save you. (Isa. 35:4)

The announcement of the liberation of God's people rushes in behind the promise of restoration of creation, even in the most desolate places:

> The desert and the parched land will be glad;
>   the wilderness will rejoice and blossom.
> Like the crocus, it will burst into bloom;
>   it will rejoice greatly and shout for joy. (Isa. 35:1 – 2)

Waters in the wilderness and streams in the desert (35:6) accompany the promise that

> the eyes of the blind be opened
>   and the ears of the deaf unstopped.
> Then will the lame leap like a deer,
>   and the mute tongue shout for joy. (Isa. 35:5 – 6)

The chapter anticipates the complete restoration of God's creation and those who live in it, both sullied by sin. The prophecy looks forward to the return to God's Promised Land with singing and joy when "sorrow and sighing will flee away" (35:10).

Jesus' work as the Great Surgeon begins that renewal. His acts, and those he accomplishes through his servants, mark the beginning of God's final and full restoration of all that is wrong in our world and in ourselves. Within the healings of the lame and the reattachment of an ear we see the future, the restoration of all creation sparking in a small and very personal act. The surgeon participates in this process of renewal. Surgery is the rainbow reminder that the broken world as we know it need not and shall not remain as it is. Surgeons offer hope that does not belong to fools but has its roots sunk firmly in the soil of God's promise, which comes to life now and will fully blossom upon the advent of the one who makes all things right and new. God enables the surgeons' work. Technology, skill, and art do not work apart from God's work.

Surgery is a violent act carried out in compassion as it challenges the destiny stamped upon a broken human frame — a frame that needs restoration. The surgeon intervenes with the hope of renewing functionality and health to the patient. Surgery offers a glimmer of the good things to come with the final advent of his kingdom that rules over all creation. Indeed, it is a present taste of that future glory, operating in the space between the fallen world and the hope of God's final redemption. The scalpel is sharp with hope, glinting brightly in the operating room and heralding the future era when God will restore all of his creation. In an imperfect way, our future hope is brought into the midst of the present agonies of our sick and broken world. The surgeon acts as the Surgeon acted.

The arrival time at the hospital is 5:00 a.m. with surgery at 7:00. The surgeon has set the schedule and arranged all the preparations. I walk forward toward tomorrow with assurance that the outcomes will be good since God is skilled as the one who fashioned and heals my body, and as the one who will restore it truly for all eternity. The surgeon and the other medical staff will be there to carry out a divine calling.

2

THE SURGERY, THE SYMPHONY,
AND SURVIVAL

C ODE BLUE!"
      While in the Intensive Care Unit after surgery, things came completely apart. I awoke from the anesthesia but could not talk since I was still intubated. Deb, my wife, was there along with my youngest daughter, Christi, and son-in-law, Josh. I was becoming distressed and over and again tapped out "• • • — — — • • •" in my wife's hand (Morse code for SOS). The multiple monitors behind my bed all displayed normal readings at first, but then the alarm sounded at the nurse's station as my heart went into ventricular tachycardia. Lying there, I could not breathe and felt that things were crashing in as my heart beat an extreme rhythm. I knew that I was dying.* The medications pulsing through my system made the frightening experience seem like being in the middle of a Picasso painting, reality distorted. The room filled with doctors and nurses, and, the next thing I knew, they shocked my heart into regular rhythm with a defibrillator. I bounced up from the bed, just like in the movies, as the painful electric shock coursed through my body. Deb and Christi were outside watching as the voltage plastered a "deer-in-the-headlights" look on my face. The doctors and nurses stood there, still and silent. In that pause, all eyes fixed on the monitors to see if a regular heart rate

---

* I later learned that ventricular tachycardia is a major cause of cardiac death.

would return. When it did, the room relaxed, the code was cleared over the public address system, and normal recovery treatment continued. One of my physicians, a specialist in cardiac electrophysiology, told me that after open-heart surgery such occurrences are rare. Before the surgery I believed that I would survive, but I also had a sense that at some point things would go wrong. God had assured me that I'd reach my destination safely, but he also warned me how difficult and dangerous the road was going to be. While grace brings us home, we're not exempt from dangers, toils, and snares.

Before the operation, I discussed the virtues of various valves, having read numerous medical journal articles and listened to the orientation my surgeon, George Kuzycz, offered me. But not once had I considered the wider circle of people who would care for me before, during, and after surgery. Everyone who prepped me for the event, explained what was going to happen, and assisted in the operating room, were specialists in their own area. They worked together collaboratively, assisting the surgeon and me as we were brought together to install a new aortic valve through open-heart surgery. Each performed a vital role in the operating theater, in ICU, and on the cardiac floor. I am alive today not only due to the skilled collaboration of the operating room staff but because of the prompt professional response of medical personnel who were not present during my surgery. They were on duty when I went into V-Tach, and in concert they brought me back from imminent death. I did not meet all the professionals who attended me, but Deborah kept a running list of everyone she met who participated in my care before and after the surgery. The bill from the hospital listed fifteen physicians who contributed in some capacity or another. The nephrologist kept close track of my kidney function, the pulmonologists worked to assure that my lung capacity would return to normal, and, when my blood platelets fell, a hematologist joined the team. My primary care physician, Mark Nelson, set the process in motion, which began with a cardiac examination and ended in the surgery. After discharge from the hospital, he once again oversaw my care as I moved forward toward a renewed future.

I remember the people who thoroughly prepped me for surgery to ensure that I would not become infected. Due to their thorough work, the care taken in the OR, and the procedures in ICU and on the cardiac floor, the cardiac unit had a zero percent infection rate, an enviable distinction. During my short stay in pre-op, the OR nurse, the physician's assistant who pulled the vein from my leg for the bypass, and the anesthesiologist oriented me to what was going to occur and explained their role in the operation. Later I discovered that my surgeon was assisted by another highly skilled and respected heart surgeon. After the surgery they transported me to the Intensive Care Unit. At the start of each shift rotation, a nurse and patient care technician were assigned to me. Their attention was constant and included every aspect of support, all timed according to plan, each step documented, with every person responsive to alerts.*

When the physicians finally wheeled me off to the cardiac unit, I soon became aware of another layer of support that was not recognized in ICU. Men and women delivered the meals we ordered from the staff in the kitchen. Daily someone came in to clean the room. Once I broke into tears upon seeing a worker replenish the hand-sanitizer, the liquid that everyone used as they entered the room and when they left to care for other patients. The worker was part of this team that labored together for the well-being of all the patients on the floor.

Each one, from the most honored to the least recognized, was a member of a great symphony orchestra that played in time and har-

---

* Later on the cardiac unit, I began to brush my teeth and was surprised that within a minute a nurse was at the door. She had a puzzled look on her face, and I asked her why she was there. The brushing action had caused the telemetry at the nurse's station to show abnormal readings and so the nurse immediately came to check on my condition. "Are you all right?" I admit that once I brushed my teeth just to find out how quick a nurse would come, but then wisely thought better of that kind of play.

mony for my health and that of the other patients. I was not in the audience, nor was I the conductor, but someone sitting on the stage watching and listening as each played their part expertly. No person attempted to drown out the participation and function of any other but each collaborated with the rest with a view to reaching a higher goal. They sought to restore my health and do no harm.

Surgery is not a solo act, but the surgeon is an expert among the practiced experts, both great and small, who collaborate to assure that the composition reaches its intended finale. Good outcomes for the one who undergoes surgery depend upon a multiplicity of players, each having learned and now faithfully playing their parts. Surgery is an intensely social undertaking, coordinated to maximize the health of the person in need of surgical intervention. Visiting home-health nurses and the medical personnel who supervised my cardiac rehabilitation also assisted the surgeon though they were far removed from the operating room. The patient yields to the surgeon and all others who seek his or her welfare. Surgery becomes an absolute surrender to the surgeon and the members of their team who are focused on the common goal of recovery after this violent intervention.

The patient's family, church, and friends join in chorus, each playing their respective roles with love and great patience. Though these post-operative caretakers may seem to have minor parts, their advocacy for the surgical patient is essential in preoperative planning, patiently waiting for the announcement of the surgery's outcomes, attending to the patient along with the hospital staff, and through the long days of strengthening the one weakened and wounded through the surgery. This attendance is no easy task as caretaking can be a long and sometimes thankless labor of love. The person who is weakened and drugged through surgery may not be aware of their need and the demands they place upon others because of their condition. The temptation for the caregiver is to return quickly to the routines and demands of daily life, leaving the surgical patient to fend for themselves. But being there, watching, helping, and acting as advocates are parts that caretakers hopefully play throughout the surgical event. They step in to speak for the patient when he or she cannot ask for help. They offer water, food, prayer, and assurance by their presence through the surgery and afterward. Suffering alone is no easy burden to carry, and attending to the one who suffers is demanding as well. Yet suffering and staying are parts of surgery. Fortunately, in 1993 the Family and Medical Leave Act came into law in the United States, allowing immediate family members to take time off work to attend to their loved ones who have a serious health condition.[4]

In his moment of greatest trial, Jesus asked the disciples to stay awake and pray with him, saying, "My soul is overwhelmed with sorrow to the point of death. Stay here and keep watch with me" (Matt. 26:38). When he returned to them, he was undoubtedly pained to find them asleep. "Couldn't you men keep watch with me for one hour?" he asked (Matt. 26:40). Afterward, the disciples deserted him (Matt. 26:56). Peter even denied him. They had failed to care for him at the moment of his greatest need. Paul, likewise, was forsaken at a critical moment in his life (2 Tim. 4:16), though he was able to say, "Luke is with me" (2 Tim. 4:11). And Paul commends the otherwise unknown Onesiphorus because, as Paul remarked, "he often refreshed me and was not ashamed of my chains. On the contrary, when he was in Rome, he searched hard for me until he found me" (2 Tim. 1:16–17). He was diligent in attending to Paul's needs while the apostle was imprisoned, and we remember him as an example to this day.

Caretaking is not easy, and sometimes caretakers fail. There is forgiveness for them, as the Lord had mercy on the disciples and Paul prayed for those who had deserted him, "May it not be held against them" (2 Tim. 4:16). But those who move in close to attend and serve imitate the sacrificial service of Christ (Mark 10:45) and serve as an example for us all.

As in God's design for all human life and activity, surgery is collaborative. Though each of us in society has a unique set of fingerprints, which differentiate us from the rest, we live together and need each other. Unsurprisingly, the Second Commandment includes the call to "love your neighbor as yourself" (Matt. 22:39; Lev. 19:18). Indeed, surgery is carried out successfully because of the good will of a town that wanted the hospital within its boundaries, the administrators who oversaw budget and expansion plans, the architects and builders who designed the surgical and other units, and the donors who helped underwrite the costs. Each surgery enjoys the support of countless people who facilitate this specialized endeavor. Surgery, from the simplest to the most complex procedure, would not be possible without the collaboration of people with diverse skills. God established the human community to work together in common cause to seek the welfare of each and of the many.

Surgery bears the fruit of broad and deep cooperation, which is God's ideal within human society. That ideal finds its best expression in Paul's understanding of the way God puts together the members of the church, each with their own particular gift that contributes to the well-being of the other and the whole (Eph. 4:11 – 13; 1 Cor. 12:12 – 26). Rather than seeking any competitive advantage, mutuality and support for each other characterize the church where the members share their lives according to God's design (Phil. 2:1 – 4). Sacrifice and service become normative as each person in the church imitates the self-humbling service of Christ (Phil. 2:5 – 11).

In the Mediterranean world of the apostle Paul, discussions about social peace often employed the image of the body as a metaphor for the harmonious functioning of society. Each person, whether slave or free, patrician or plebian, would do their part to contribute to the whole. These discussions were designed to keep those in power on the top of the social pyramid and to assure that the subordinate members of society would maintain their place. Although slaves were essential members of society, the thought was that they should not revolt. Paul adopts yet subverts this language in 1 Corinthians 12:12 – 26, underscoring the honor given to each member (12:22 – 24). Every person has an essential role that benefits the rest, no matter their social status (12:14–21, 25–26). Paul lays out God's ideal for society and offers the world an example in the way the church functions, or at least should function. The church should not simply adopt the competitive and individualistic standards of the world. So, at its best, the collaborative society of the medical community reflects this same mutuality amidst the diversity that makes surgery successful for the individual in need of this drastic intervention. But if the group becomes dysfunctional, the patient will suffer through mismanagement, lack of attention, infection, and neglect.

Christians are aware of God's involvement in the church but often do not recognize the way God providentially works through society. In his first letter, Peter speaks of the *anthrōpinē ktisei* (1 Pet. 2:13), a Greek expression notoriously difficult to translate into English (rendered "human authority" in the NIV). The first term means "human" but the second commonly refers to what God creates or establishes. In the context of 1 Peter 2:13–17, the apostle refers to the institutions of the state that, while human, bear the stamp of divine establishment. But the term was also used to refer to the founding of cities in the ancient world. However we understand and translate the second term in this expression, which may refer to either human or divine institutional establishment, it is "for the Lord's sake" (2:13) that we show due honor to political leaders. Although Christians may be deemed "foreigners and exiles" in society (2:11), they understand that God is the Creator of all (1 Pet. 4:19). He providentially oversees the course of human history and assures the life of both individuals and society (Acts 17:26–28). God's providence brings us together into collaborative labors, and the intense, skilled cooperation within surgery becomes a pinnacle example of the social fabric God weaves. This orchestra produces a magnificent symphony.

This ideal is not always realized in our world where sin and self-interest often take primary place over attempts to assure the welfare of all through seeking the good for the other. A surgical suite could become a venue of discord and conflict if strong egos battle and scorn others. Workers can fail to undertake their role with any moral conviction, seeking only to punch in and out while not recognizing how important their labor is for the whole enterprise to succeed. If the medicines and equipment are not available due to neglect, in the end the one needing surgery suffers deeply. As the medieval monasteries became havens of order in a chaotic and dangerous world, and as the Shaker communities in Kentucky offered a refuge of harmony, good labor, health, and craftsmanship in the midst of the hunger and dangers of the West, so the surgical suite and the hospital where it resides should be a model of harmonious collaboration whose goal is to establish health and wholeness.

While in recovery, I received visitors, flowers, cards, and emails from God's people near and far who assured me of their daily prayers as I went through and recovered from surgery. The community of God's people was at work on their knees, in silent seated moments, with lifted hands and voices, privately and publically. One of the ministers from our church brought me a prayer shawl, knitted by women in the church who had prayed for the health of the person who would receive it as they looped each strand. I have never been more aware of the prayers offered for my health and for my family, prayers that buoyed us up at this moment of crisis and healing. Months after my own hospital stay, my wife, Deb, became a kidney donor, and she and her recipient were joined together with family, friends, church members, and colleagues in a concert of prayer. We were not alone but part of that great company of God's people whose prayers the Lord hears (1 Pet. 3:12, quoting Ps. 34:15). We were conscious of God's presence and care, and knew that he was upholding us in response to the faithful intercession on our behalf. The dangers of surgery were overcome, we saw everything fall into place, with questions answered, fears subdued, and health restored. God answered.

During recovery, the visits of friends and ministers are especially welcome. They reflect a thoughtful response to Jesus' affirmation, "I was sick and you looked after me" (Matt. 25:36, 45). Taking care of the sick in Jesus' day included more than stopping by a hospital bed. It involved a deeper level of caretaking that the person in a modern hospital in the West does not require. In other parts of the world, where medical care is thin and resources scarce, such caretaking can make the difference between life and death. Those who come bring essential medicines, funds, and food. But the language of Matthew 25:36 is not limited to such extreme care but suggests all the ways that we may look after another person and respond to their needs. The visit is a sign of support, care, and solidarity for the person who has undergone surgery and for the rest who devote themselves to caretaking.

During the first weeks after both my wife and I returned from the hospital, people from the church mobilized to bring us meals, expressing their care as Jesus had instructed. Social support from others in all its aspects contributes to a person's recovery after surgery.[5] Solitude is crushing, while in community we are strong. Just showing up and being there become a source of strength and recovery for the patient and also their caretakers.

In our day, short visits that focus on the needs of the person who underwent surgery are welcome, whereas long visits and talk centering on the normal affairs of life are not always helpful. The visitor's presence is an assurance that others have not forgotten. A touch can strengthen, but a strong embrace can cause pain. Loud talk can leave the patient longing for refuge, whereas soft and assuring speech brings comfort and assurance. A few people whose visits are brief and well-timed are more welcome than a large number of people who have little sense of where they are or the purpose of their visit. Heavy scents of cologne or perfume are not always pleasant for the person recovering, whereas prayers offered up and a soft touch bring a welcome fragrance of hope and healing.

Clergy visits are especially encouraging, as the presence of a minister of the gospel stands for the presence of the whole church. Two ministers of our congregation and the chaplain from my college visited me, bringing the prayers and support of a larger body with them.

Partaking the Lord's table together can be especially healing and hopeful as this act turns the patient's eyes on Jesus Christ, the one who was crucified and is risen. The presence of others gives hope, as the patient not only knows that they are cared for but is enabled to look out beyond themselves again to the wider affairs of life. And the ministry of others helps the patient turn again to God in faith in the midst of their troubles and fears. There is healing in these visits.

My family became members of this healing community that walked through surgery with me. My wife, daughters, granddaughter, son-in-law, and brother were present with me, and I was left on my own in the hospital for only a few nights toward the end of my stay. My brother, Charles, drove down from Minnesota, and Gillian and Penelope, my eldest daughter and granddaughter, flew out from New York the week before, and again when I emerged from surgery. The second visit was a surprise, which prompted me to ask my wife, "Are things really that bad?" But they came to support me, not to witness my demise. During the recovery period, our youngest daughter ministered the gospel to me, the same good news we had taught her over the years. She led me spiritually, an expression of honor as we exchanged our customary roles. My son-in-law, Joshua, supported my wife, daughters, and me through his constant presence and willingness to take on any helpful task he could. While they propped me up, they fought their own fears and questions, loneliness and despair, which my unknown destiny foisted upon them. They gathered together for strength and welcomed every person who inquired about their well-being and prayed for them. My family needed the stabilizing that the medical personnel and friends could bring. They were made fast to my bed in the operating room and ICU, towed behind my reversals and recovery, and buoyed by the support others offered them.

The family watched over me, responded to my requests and questions, and served as another link between me and the medical staff. When doctors or nurses explained the various procedures and findings, Deb, an advanced practice nurse, listened with me and interpreted what they said. Her medical knowledge helped us understand the challenges I faced after surgery. While recovering in the hospital and at home, she selflessly cared for me with the expertise and experience of her nursing profession, all expressed with the deepest love. Years ago, Deb assisted Stephen Hawking* as a personal nurse, and now she turned her skills to my care. A key reason for my speedy recovery was the support I received from my family. They were there and I was not alone. Love and support mark our family, but the surgery brought out the stunning colors and warmth of family solidarity. Conversely, a fractured family would have broken my spirit and fought against recovery, but wholeness in the family brought health. The commands to honor father and mother, the call to love our spouse and our children, were all present as part of the surgical process (Col. 3:18 – 24; 1 Pet. 3:7). This community support is the concrete and daily manifestation of God's ideal of unity within all human society.

Caretaking is not easy work. It demands time, mental focus, active research, and sometimes physical exertion. There are long hours that stretch into late nights and mornings. This is good and essential work, but it is not easy work. Caretakers can become physically and emotionally exhausted at the very moment when they are called upon to be supportive and strong. The dailyness of caring for another demands resolve and selflessness that may, at times, be hard to muster, especially as the caretaker's own needs may be left unattended. Caring for another person can be a source of great joy and satisfaction, and it brings no regrets. But it is not easy, something that needy patients may forget. Caretakers need caretaking in the form of thanks, relief by others, nourishment, and rest. Jesus, the Greatest Caretaker, understood this and sought relief for himself and his disciples: "Then, because so many people were coming and going

---

* Hawking was the Lucasian Professor of Mathematics at the University of Cambridge. He has Lou Gehrig's disease (ALS), which has left him with minimal muscle control. His popular book *A Brief History of Time* (New York: Bantam, 1988) became an international bestseller.

that they did not even have a chance to eat, he said to them, 'Come with me by yourselves to a quiet place and get some rest'" (Mark 6:31). But sometimes rest gets interrupted (Mark 6:32–34).

After undergoing V-Tach and the subsequent shock of defibrillation, my daughter Christi sat by me in ICU. Deeply concerned for my well-being, she prayed earnestly for my survival and health. She was frightened and cried out to God on my behalf. In those early hours of the morning the Lord opened her eyes, as if Elisha had prayed, "Open his eyes, LORD, so that he may see" (2 Kings 6:17, 20), and the host of heaven was revealed. Christi saw two strong angels, standing at the head of my ICU bed, protecting and upholding me. Another stood by her side, both of us being in their care. At that moment, the Lord spoke to her heart saying, "He will be okay." My wife also remarked how she sensed another invisible supernatural presence in the room during that critical time in ICU. Hearing these stories later, I was humbled to tears, realizing that God's mighty angels do indeed minister to those who are heirs of salvation (Heb. 1:14). God promises his constant presence (Heb. 13:5). Up to that point, I had seen doctors, nurses, and patient-care technicians walk up and down the halls and into my room. The phlebotomists came before dawn to draw blood, and the X-ray technicians took multiple pictures of my lungs for the pulmonologists. Family and visitors came, flowers and cards arrived from friends and colleagues. But there was more going on in the halls and rooms of the hospital, that place of surgical intervention and healing. Christ and his angels were present with their strength and protection, the unannounced visitors who came to bring healing and restore health. Surgery is a social event, but those who gather round near and far are not only human but supernatural and divine. Divine society includes God the Father, the Risen Christ, the Spirit of God, and the company of God's mighty angels. They arrived for the surgery and remained afterward. They managed the outcomes, which in my case were good.

Six months after my surgery my role switched from patient to caretaker. My wife, Deb, became a kidney donor for Eileen, a missionary in the Dominican Republic and friend of ours for nearly forty years. (More about this in chapter 4.) Deb had set the bar very high with her selfless attendance to my needs while in the hospital and during the weeks and months after returning home. She was present and observant through the long hospital nights and vigilant in her oversight after my homecoming. Now her care fell into my hands, and I wondered if I could manage the task with the diligence and joy she had displayed, although I knew that I could not match her medical skill and insight. Fortunately, she was climbing stairs quickly and was not nearly as fragile as I had been after open-heart surgery. But she had a time of considerable worry in the hospital when her remaining kidney did not appear to be functioning fully at first, a post-operative problem that passed in the early morning hours. She also experienced severe pain and gastrointestinal upset upon the return home. How could I troubleshoot and liaise with the hospital medical staff to find her the relief that she needed? I quickly discovered that her care for me had mapped the way to follow. The path was already laid out, her model being True North on the road of caretaking. By her daily example I had learned afresh what it meant to be a good caretaker and companion. I understood more deeply and could see more clearly the meaning of community by following the score written by her life. *Imitatio* is a principle way that we learn. Watching and listening to others, and seeking to follow their movements and speech, is part of our educational journey from childhood through later years. Christians are called to watch Christ's life and engage in the *imitatio Christi*, while God's acts are laid down as patterns for us to follow as well in the *imitatio Dei*. But the life of another person may also become an example to follow, a pattern for community life and good deeds (1 Cor. 4:6; 11:1; Eph. 5:1; Phil. 3:17; 1 Thess. 1:6).

Surgery is a wondrous celebration of the way the human community can come together to accomplish a good that one person alone could never undertake. The best surgical theater is one where skilled professionals endeavor to work together in concert to promote the patient's health and safety. A team in conflict can diminish the effec-

Callslip Request   5/23/2016 8:12:23 AM

Item Location: stx
Call Number: 261.561 G7961
Enumeration:
Copy Number:
Chronology:
Year:
Item Barcode:

Title: Scalpel and the cross : a theology of
       surgery / Gene L. Green.
Author: Green, Gene L.,

Patron Name: Michael Cox
Patron Group: UBReg
Patron Barcode:

5 9 2 0 0 4

Reason if item is not available:
__At Bindery: Seeking next available
__Item Charged Out: Seeking next available
__Damaged: Seeking next available
__Local Circulation Only: Seeking next availab
__Missing/Not on Shelf: Seeking next available
__Noncirculation item: Seeking next available

Reassignment History:
None

Patron comment:

Request date: 5/23/2016 04:18 AM
Request number: 53746

5 3 7 4 6

Pick Up Location if Local Request:

tive work of others, bringing detriment to the surgical patient. A coordinated team of individuals helps ensure that the recovery will be smooth and without incident. If medical staff are not attentive to a post-operative patient's needs, their neglect may put the surgeon's work at risk and jeopardize the recovery process. In some hospitals, staffing has become so short that caregivers are unable to offer optimal care and, therefore, may miss the signs of distress that often follow surgery. No member of the hospital staff should think of their job as a mere bureaucratic duty to be performed at the lowest standard possible. From food service to cleaning, each person's work is essential for the health of the patient. The support from friends and family contributes strongly to the surgical patient's recovery. Family tensions need to be left behind, allowing forgiveness and cooperation to take their place. And the prayers of God's people are heard by him, and he will listen and respond. He convokes the company gathered for surgery.

I am happily recovering and gaining strength, and Deb has returned to her work after surgery. But for some, the outcome is different, as it could have been for Deb and me. Those who call upon the Lord can lay there or stand as Stephen did saying, "Lord Jesus, receive my spirit" (Acts 7:59). Some die under the hope of the blessed resurrection (1 Thess. 4:13 – 18; 1 Cor. 15). Their link with divine society is not broken, even in death, and they continue as members of God's family (Matt. 22:32). Surgery is "an act of authority on destiny," as Leriche said. But the final outcomes are in the hands of God. The surgeon and the whole company of medical personnel, family, and faithful friends do their part in the surgery, but the Great Surgeon is the one whom we trust ultimately. He brings life where there is death and will wipe away every tear (Rev. 21:4; 7:17). He can and does keep us in life and in death.

3

SURGERY FOR
THE BODY AND SOUL

M AJOR SURGERIES BRING A PERSON INTO INTIMATE DIALOG WITH the fundamental questions of human existence. Emergency surgery to save a life or medically necessary surgery to correct a life-threatening problem are events that lead patients and their families to reflect on life and death, wills and disability, the meaning of being or the plans for the future in the absence of the one who underwent an unsuccessful surgery. Such deep reflection does not necessarily precede or follow all surgeries as some modern medical interventions have become minor procedures that do not bring a person face-to-face with the ultimate realities of human existence. The more major the surgery, the more likely a person is to ask the "big questions" of life, although a reflective person undergoing a minor intervention may find that the event triggers thoughts about the relative frailty of human existence. And, indeed, all surgeries carry risk. These thoughts may be positive or negative and extremely distressing.

People who undergo cardiac surgery often remark how the event brought changes at the deepest level of their life. Those who have defined themselves in terms of the labor they carry out may, after the surgery, find their physical abilities dramatically diminished. They cannot function as they had before surgery and now question their worth and the purpose of their existence. Many people enter into a period of depression after open-heart surgery. A person's concept of self and their labor morphs as surgery exposes weaknesses in the human frame and sometimes leaves the patient in a less-than-perfect state. Surgery may impose new limitations on a person's activity or underscore the ravages that age wrecks upon the body. The period after surgery for many becomes a time of soul searching, especially if the surgery acted as an imposition of authority upon a very dreadful destiny. The patient is snatched from disaster, bringing him or her to contemplate the course of their life up to the present, the nature of their future, and the ultimate issues of life and death. The "big picture" fixes the attention as the daily routines become altered, sometimes permanently.

I had not expected that my surgery would be anything more than a medical intervention with a period of recovery afterward, at least under the best-case scenario. But something occurred at a deeper spiritual and existential level that was not anticipated. I knew beforehand that open-heart surgery brought with it risks, and prudence dictated taking the necessary steps to assure the well-being of my family should I perish in surgery or recovery. My wife and I had new wills drawn up and signed. I sat down with her, and then my two daughters, to discuss what life would look like without my presence, support, and income. The house would be paid off, they should get on with their lives after mourning my demise, each should look to the Lord Jesus and rely on each other to carry them through. All very morbid yet necessary. Our discussions were warm yet distressing, hopeful yet realistic. We could not control the outcomes, but we could make wise plans, and I wanted to offer the best council I could as a potentially departing husband and father. Yet we all moved forward in the hope that none of the talks and provisions would be really necessary.*

After coming through the surgery and the initial crisis in recovery,

---

* Such talks can lay good foundations for future days when such provisions will be necessary.

I had the keen awareness that God was carrying me through this very difficult time. Somehow I knew that not only my family but friends elsewhere were holding me up in prayer, interceding on my behalf. The Lord was present throughout the operation on my heart and was also watching over me through recovery. Through the pain, my first thoughts were ones of deep gratitude and joy. I had not been forgotten by God or others. The solidarity of this divine and human support brought me level upon level of deep gratitude, sometimes expressed in ways that seemed maudlin. But it was difficult to contain the wellspring of gratitude to God, to those who helped with the surgery and recovery, and to every other person who supported me through the time. Each had given a gift that was undeserved, and their gift meant life to me. How could I not express profound thanks to a surgeon who has added years to my earthly existence? The thanks were effusive and somewhat embarrassing for the recipient, but heartfelt and sincere.

When Jesus healed the ten lepers, only one who knew his unworthiness turned and thanked him (Luke 17:11 – 19). Jesus had instructed them to go and show themselves to the priests (17:14), as prescribed by the Old Testament Law (Lev. 14). But the Samaritan would not have been welcomed into the temple in Jerusalem. He turned, however, and offered something far better than what Jesus prescribed. He returned to thank the one who was responsible for his healing. The lame man at the temple gate was healed in the name of Jesus. He jumped up and went "walking and jumping, and praising God," entering into his presence (Acts 3:8). Surgery is not simply an act that seeks to improve the destiny of the one who needs the intervention but also puts a responsibility on the shoulders of the healed person. His or her part is to offer proper thanks, both to the physician and the Physician.

The surgeon's intervention is intended to improve a person's life, even through the drastic measures of opening the body with a scalpel and sewing the person back together, extracting diseased and malfunctioning body parts, and sometimes replacing them with prosthetics, either biological or mechanical. This dramatic invasion of the body reminds us of the way God's salvation embraces the whole of a person's being, both body and soul. Indeed, the very word used for eternal and spiritual salvation, *sōzō*, may refer in other contexts to the healing of the body (as in James 5:15). While historically in Western thought we have maintained a sharp distinction between a person's body and mind, or body and soul, the biblical view of personhood is more holistic and embraces all that a person is. So, for example, the Christian hope is not simply immortality of the soul but also the resurrection of the body (1 Cor. 15; 1 Thess. 4:13 – 18). God is out to save the whole person and not just part of our being. The surgical process, especially major surgery, brings with it reflections on human existence and matters of the heart, not simply the body. The surgeon operated on my heart as God operated on my heart.

During recovery, I was surprised to discover that my conscience became troubled. As I lay in bed, I thought about a number of actions, attitudes, and words that had not been for the well-being of others but had caused harm. I was deeply disturbed by these thoughts yet knew that God was mending my heart, not just physically, as he continued to speak to me about the way I was living. He brought sin to light, and before him, in the hospital, he led me to repentance and confession. The spiritual cleansing was deep, surgical, and quite surprising. While I knew that one's emotions could be affected deeply by heart surgery, I did not anticipate the spiritual journey that would bring me to the heart of God's concern for my eternal well-being.

I should have remembered Jesus' words to the paralyzed man whom he healed (Luke 5:17 – 26). His friends had brought the man to Jesus but could not get near to him since a large crowd had gathered in the house where Jesus taught. They climbed up to the roof, carrying the lame man with them, and then opened the tiles to let the man down in front of Jesus. Jesus' first words to the man were, "Friend, your sins are forgiven." After that, he healed the man so he could walk (5:20, 24 – 25).

Healing of the body is the physical counterpoint to the true surgical healing God accomplishes in bringing a person to repentance and offering forgiveness. Human need is not simply physical but spiritual. So, James says, "And the prayer offered in faith will make the sick person well; the Lord will raise them up. If they have sinned, they will be forgiven" (James 5:15). Surgery examines and corrects the inner workings of the body but also opens the patient to the deeper spiritual surgical intervention by the Lord. If surgery brings questions about the direction of a person's life to center stage, what could be more important in this scene than one's spiritual state? God is the Great Surgeon who does what no earthly surgeon is able to do since he leaves no part of a person outside his intervention and grace.

At the heart of this question we discover the cross of Christ. Christ's body was broken as he bore the sins of each and every person (1 John 2:2). As Peter said, " 'He himself bore our sins' in his body on the cross, so that we might die to sins and live for righteousness" (1 Pet. 2:24). As he echoes Isaiah 53:4 and 12, Peter also includes a reflection on Isaiah 53:5, "By his wounds we are healed." His sacrifice and death for sin offers true healing for every person, the ones lost like sheep gone astray (1 Pet. 2:25; Isa. 53:6). The wounds Christ endured were those inflicted on the Shepherd of our souls and not only our bodies. Surgery seeks to do good and bring healing, yet it is a violent act. Thus it reminds us of the violence Christ endured for the health of our soul as well as our body. The controlled violence the surgical patient experiences is for their good, as the violence done to Christ on the cross was for us and our salvation. Surgery leads us by the hand into a deeper understanding of the cross of Christ and to the heart of the mystery of how God has chosen to save and redeem people. The bloody and painful wounds inflicted through surgery for our well-being are a close human analogy to the harm done to Christ who was nailed to the cross for our redemption. The patient and surgeon see the gleam of the cross in the operating room.

Whoever undergoes an operation needs to take a moment to prepare spiritually before the event. Seeking support and prayer from a minister along with family and friends will help prep the patient for what will be a spiritual journey. Prayers and counsel from Scripture serve as sustaining food for this long journey. We do not live by bread alone (Matt. 4:4). Preparation for surgery may be a means of avoiding the detour into despair, which some experience as they realize that they have become weakened and their life may change in ways not expected. After the surgery, the patient needs opportunities to talk about concerns and fears as they work through the meaning of the event for their soul and their future life. Ministers, Christian family and friends, and counselors should be available to talk about the life issues exposed by the bright lights of the operation. Surgery is a "time out" in the game, a moment to consider strategies and approaches to life that we do not attend to in the normal rush and pressure of modern life. And, in the end, the agonies of surgery bring us back to Jesus, leading us to the cross in repentance — since he died for our sins — and hope, since the crucified one was raised from the dead. God's concern is for the whole person, not just the body. Surgery leads to the core questions of human life. And there is hope here.

4

REPLACEMENT PARTS

THE SURGERY LANDED ME WITH THE QUESTION OF WHETHER TO opt for a mechanical or bioprosthetic heart valve, a decision anyone in my position must make. The technology at present does not present a clear, unequivocal choice since mechanical valves tend to produce clotting and so the patients with this kind of prostheses must take an anticoagulant drug, most commonly Coumadin, throughout their life. Coumadin, also known as Warfarin, brings with it the danger of prolonged bleeding. Minor injuries can turn into major crises. As one surgeon remarked, "Coumadin itself is a condition." For me, it would mean the end of cycling, my favorite sport, since a head injury from a fall could cause intracranial bleeding, even if I were wearing a helmet. On the other side, while biological valves do not tend to produce clotting, the durability of the bioprosthetic is nowhere near as great as mechanical valves. Should the patient live long enough, it will require replacement. The average life-span of the bioprosthetics varies, but somewhere between a decade and twenty years may be expected. Current designs hold the promise of greater valve longevity, but the Holy Grail of a durable bioprosthetic remains out of reach. In the end, patient longevity averages about the same whatever kind of valve a person chooses.[6] Lifestyle issues and the possibility of reoperation become major considerations in the decision-making process.

The patient is left to choose on the basis of oral reports and basic information packets written at near high-school level. Issues of lifestyle and life-expectancy rise rapidly from the horizon. Life will change, but how is partially bound to this choice. I have the advantage of being married to a healthcare professional who helped me access some of the best literature available on the topic, but not everyone can obtain this wealth of scientific research available through medical libraries. Patients are often called upon to make choices before surgery in a timely manner or even in a rush, frequently without having all the information at the ready to make a safe and solid decision. They and their families can make wiser decisions that they will not regret if they have adequate information readily at hand and take advantage of it. Unfortunately, choosing our next car would be easier given the detailed information available compared with that offered by physicians and hospitals about surgical procedures. Many hospitals publish a large amount of educational information on their websites, but what they supply are often basic explanations, which are recycled over and over again on websites dealing with the same issue. The duties of health professionals are not simply procedural but educational. And it cannot be otherwise if the medical community wants patients and their families to take responsibility for their own healthcare. Moreover, in our information age the gap between the seriousness of surgical procedures and patient education offered before undertaking them is strikingly odd. Full disclosure and information access are essential, not just for legal protection for the healthcare industry but for moral reasons. Strangely enough, some patients do not want much information, trusting rather in the judgment of their physician and not seeking to be an informed and responsible patient. Very odd, indeed, especially for Christians whose faith is woven with threads of personal responsibility overlapping those of divine providence.

On the other hand, decisions made in partial darkness and uncertain outcomes will always accompany the technology and skill of the surgical art, despite the best information available. Not everything in a surgical procedure is predictable, even with the best longitudinal studies in hand. But this is the stuff of life with God, where understanding and clarity walk together with confusion and darkness. Multiple acts of faith arise in the middle of all this, each done with good information, each undertaken with inadequate understanding. We trust in the surgeons and their skill, and trust in God for the final outcomes. The synergy of human responsibility and divine agency hammer me back down into the heart of our faith. Surgery necessarily entails faith, but grace brings us safe through waters that chop and churn.

I opted for a biological valve, coming full circle after reading and consultation. At first a carbon valve had seemed the preferred option. The decision is not reversible since there are no refunds and no exchanges in the first thirty days. The week before surgery, my family and I took our granddaughter to a small, local zoo. In the throes of the valve decision, my family made numerous humorous comments as we drew near the pigs and cows. I was not ready for those remarks and rapidly changed the subject. But now I can look the pig square in the eye and thank him, my brother.* Medtronics, the company that bioengineered the valve, calls it a Mosaic Ultra Porcine Heart Valve. They sent me a wallet card with its model and serial number. But even with the technical name and ID number, I know where it came from. A pig gave his valve so that I may have more years on this earth than my present valve would allow. A sacrifice was made so that I might live and that my quality of life might be improved. In Homer's *Odyssey,* Odysseus' men were better off after having been transformed into pigs by Circe and then turned back into men, so my life is prolonged and improved through this union with a fellow creature.[7] When changed again, they became "younger than ever, taller by far, more handsome to the eye." Unfortunately,

---

* The pig may have been female and, therefore, my sister. The male gender may be inappropriate here, and my use of it should be viewed as no more than generic. I would be equally happy with a valve donated by a gilt, sow, or boar.

my porcine valve did not produce the same extraordinary results, but my life was lengthened and enriched.

The creature who was sacrificed is also a kinsman who came before me in God's creation (Gen. 1:24–25). He was brought forth from the earth as was the first human. We share a common source and the one Creator formed us. We were designed so similarly that, with just a bit of creative engineering, we can swap some parts. The pig is more than bacon and chops to me, but a fellow creature of the Creator who stood before me in God's plan and who sacrificed his life for me. Pigs have been dirty and tasty, cute and clever in my culinary, literary, and comic world. They sometimes become domestic pets who exhibit canine-like intelligence, as the movie *Babe* humorously reminded us. But this pig is close to my heart. Indeed, my heart's every beat depends completely on him, testimony of our shared life together. And as he is now, so I will be some day. But not now, not this day. He has made sure of that, and I am grateful to this brother creature and our common Creator.

The sacrifice made for my life echoes that greatest sacrifice Christ Jesus made on the cross. The despised and rejected one died for me and for all. Who was more lowly than Christ, the one despised and rejected (Isa. 53:3)? And what creature shares the ignominy of the pig? As Jesus cried on the cross as one forsaken (Mark 15:34), he gave his life as a ransom for many (Mark 10:45). He bled and he suffered and died. Offered wine mixed with gall, a bitter concoction to ease his suffering, he denied it (Matt. 27:34).[8] He entrusted himself fully to the Father as he gave the last breath. And three days later he rose from the dead. His death facilitated the implantation of a new heart (Ezek. 11:19; 18:31; 36:26), the surgery predicted by the prophet Ezekiel and promised by Jesus. But the act of healing surgery also required something from me, pain and bleeding that cut deep, down to the very bone and soul. The surgery itself is a reminder of the wounds Christ endured and constitutes a call to change, as a painful act of repentance.

The new birth and life Christ offers far exceed the hopeful

statistical analyses that guide evidence-based surgical practice. His promises are sure and firm, the outcomes not in question, the percentages always at the maximum. His healing and implantation do not last for a decade or two but hold the promise of eternity. The surgeon can make a stand against death and disease, inserting a prosthetic to prolong or better life, but the cuts the Great Surgeon endured bring benefits to the patient that transcend the grave. Surgery has its risks, even death. But even in this there is no sting, only the hope of sharing his resurrection (1 Cor. 15).

Prosthetics of any type focus our attention on the relationship between human technology and divine biological design. Whether the prosthetic is a heart valve or an artificial joint, each is an attempt to mimic the design of the original biological component. A "prosthetic" is something added to the human frame (the term comes from the Greek *prosthēkē*, which means "an addition" or "an appendage"). We use prosthetics when damage has occurred to the original body part, such as a calcified aortic valve that does not open fully, or if a part was missing or poorly developed from birth. We most often think of mechanical devices, like an artificial heart or a carbon heart valve, as being true prosthetics. But a prosthetic device may be biological as well, such as an engineered bovine or porcine valve that has been manipulated and treated in such a way that it may serve, in its modified state, as a replacement for an original human body part. A transplant, like transplanted heart, kidney, hand, or even face, is similar to a prosthetic in that it is an addition to a person's own biology. The technology involved for implantation in the subject does not include bioengineering but simply matching donor and recipient, surgery, and the administration of anti-rejection drugs.

The quest to imitate as closely as possible the divine design of human anatomy is one that shows no sign of slowing. In this arena, technology promises some of its greatest victories. Prosthetics have, unsurprisingly, become part of the stuff of science fiction as we admire Luke Skywalker's artificial wrist and hand that replaced the one Darth Vader cut off with a light saber. In *I, Robot*, the movie adaptation of an Isaac Asimov's short story, we discover that Del Spooner, played by Will Smith, has a prosthetic arm. In these visions, the prosthetic device is as good as or even better than original equipment. While this remains the Holy Grail for all prosthetics, most can only mimic the original parts of the human frame and do not promise the same functionality as healthy human biology. The artificial heart is severely prone to rejection, the mechanical heart valve tends to damage red blood cells and encourage the formation of dangerous blood clots, the bioprosthetic heart valve has a limited lifespan. Some prosthetics, however, have become extremely well designed and relatively easy to install, such as the replacement of a person's cataracts with a plastic prosthetic. We can only wonder at these great technological advances, yet at the same time our awe of the original deepens. The Master Designer did a most excellent job. We are indeed wonderfully made (Ps. 139:14).

The intersection of biology and technology begins before the implantation of the prosthetic. During open-heart surgery the surgeon attaches the person to a heart-lung machine ("the pump"), then stops the patient's heart. Through this cardiopulmonary bypass, the pump takes over the job of circulating blood and oxygen through a person's body while the surgeon operates on a heart that has ceased to beat. The body temperature lowers to the point of hypothermia as the temporary prosthetic takes over the vital functions of the human body. The pump maintains life in the body, including the brain, so that the surgeon may operate in a field that is motionless and bloodless. Drugs that suppress consciousness and eliminate pain facilitate this delicate interface of human and machine. The advanced technology, however, could not live on its own but only serves a supporting role. Humanity, in all its frailty, maintains the honored place in this temporary union whose end goal is the restoration and independence of the person's organs. While this sustaining technology inspires awe, the ability of the frail human frame to endure the mechanical interface and then be restored to functionality is the true wonder. The pump can never live, but the human can. Yet a few minutes without the pump would cause the patient to lose their grip on the slender string of life. There is weakness here, the kind that Jesus experienced in his incarnation (Heb. 2:17). That life could be lost and did end abruptly (2 Cor. 13:4). But the Father and Creator restored his life. Likewise, the patient's heart begins to beat on its own once reconnected to the circulatory system and shocked back into normal rhythm. Sutures hold as blood flows. The sleeper has awakened.

God endowed human beings with the ability to make things with a variety of increasingly refined tools, as Tubal-Cain in Genesis 4:22 "forged all kinds of tools out of bronze and iron." The human technological craft imitates the character of God whom we know as the one who "created the heavens and the earth" (Gen. 1:1). The Creator formed the first human out of the dust of the ground (Gen. 2:7; 1:26–31) and endowed that primal person with life. He created humanity in his image (Gen. 1:26), and with that came the longing to fashion and create things, to employ technology for good ends. Humans are adept imitators, a trait of human character that allows for the development of human personality, communication and community, and production of all kinds. The *imitatio Dei* is not limited to the imitation of God's character (1 Pet. 1:15) but embraces his act and art in design. However, the fruit of imitation, human technology, bows before the original. While mechanical hearts and valves are some of the highest expressions of this endowment, they come short of reproducing the character and complexity of the real thing. The surgeon works along this horizon, seeking to use technological innovations that do not have the full functionality, durability, or even harmonious synergy with other organs as do the original body parts. And yet we urge the creators of these technologies and the surgeons who utilize them to move forward and experiment, even in the face of failure and imperfection. Humans possess a wondrous depth of creativity and skill, but we cannot duplicate what God has created. Yet the impulse to engage in the *imitatio Dei*, especially for healing and bettering the human condition, is sewn within our nature as those who bear his image, the *imago Dei*.

The place where biology and technology most tightly intertwine is the use and formation of bioprosthetics, whether for heart valves or in the reconstruction of an abdominal wall or pericardium using a bioprosthetic mesh. Harvesting animal tissue products for these prosthetics raises ethical issues regarding the value of animal life, animal rights, and our relationship to the animal world. To be sure, as carnivores we understand that the animal world is for our use and benefit whether we eat a ham sandwich, sushi, or fried chicken (Gen. 9:2 – 3). Animals were the source for clothing (Gen. 3:21) and sacrifices (Gen. 4:3 – 4). However, some people point us back to God's original design when he provided a vegetarian diet (Gen. 1:29; 2:15 – 16). They could argue that we unnecessarily exploit animals by taking body parts from them for human use and that this is unethical. But the broad assent in Scripture in favor of using animals for human benefit, including food, opens an ethical door for harvesting animal parts for medical use.

Current concerns about how chickens are raised in factory farms, however, and the way cattle are slaughtered in abattoirs again drive ethics into the center of the discussion about our relationship to animals.[9] While vegetarians might be the only ones to take a stand against the consumption of animal flesh, all of us should be concerned that our use of fellow creatures does not degenerate into abuse.[10] We cannot cause undue suffering to animals without diminishing our role as caretakers of this world's goods, whether living or inanimate. We are not simply consumers. The same holds for engineering bioprosthetics. How are the cows, pigs, and horses treated who are then slaughtered to harvest tissue for human bioprosthetics? And how do we properly honor these creatures who, as we, were formed out of the dust of the earth and who came before us as elders in God's world (Gen. 1:24 – 25)? We cannot simply use Brother Pig or Sister Cow for our ends without acknowledging their rightful place in God's creation and the sacrifice they make for our well-being.

Native American Christian theology, more than traditional Western theology, understands the union and continuity between all creatures of the Creator. The late Richard Twiss, a Rosebud Lakota and founder of Wiconi International, emphasized that we are fellows with the animals in God's creation. "Native Americans," he stated, "see themselves as a part of the whole creation. They have long perceived and pursued a balanced relationship between man and the environment — a partnership of equality and respect."[11] Twiss commented on the relationship between humans and the animal world saying, "Native people have respected nature, killing only what they needed for food, clothing or shelter."[12] Indeed, Native American Christian theology is infused with a deep ecological consciousness that emphasizes "responsible stewardship of God's creation," a position that Western theologians are beginning to adopt. The world is not simply for our use and abuse. While Native American Christian theology would not oppose bioprosthetics, it does encourage respectful and honorable recognition of the sacrifice another creature has undergone for our well-being. A Native American view of our relation to the rest of creation begins by saying with the Lakota, "Mitakuye Oyasin," that is, "All my relatives."[13] We can acknowledge our creatureliness without denying our own responsibility in this world as those formed in the image of God. Our present state and our ultimate destiny are bound inseparably with the rest of God's creation, as Paul says, "For the creation was subjected to frustration, not by its own choice, but by the will of the one who subjected it, in hope that the creation itself will be liberated from its bondage to decay and brought into the freedom and glory of the children of God" (Rom. 8:20 – 21).

For my part, I thank Brother or Sister Pig for granting me life. He or she gave the utmost so that my heart could continue to beat. Like the lamb, this pig has become a representation of Christ, the despised one who died so that all may live. The animal who allows my heart to beat is indeed noble, an innocent slaughtered so I could continue my journey. The insertion of his valve into my heart was a sacred surgical act that calls me to honor my fellow's sacrifice. The creature who gave it up for me turns my head back to the sacrifice of

Christ. And the technology that made this union possible is nothing less than an imitation of God's creative act in taking one thing to form another. Yet this technology needs to be used with due recognition of the rights and place of the creatures who inhabit the world God created. Whether we are looking at mechanical or biological prosthetics for surgical implantation, there is a divine wonder here as they are fitted to function as best they can until the day of our resurrection. But there is also a call here for responsible use of technology and for deep humility before the skill and art of the Creator. Given this, patients are not simply passive recipients of the surgeon's craft and the prosthetic gift but participants in the ethical issues surrounding surgery.

Six months after my surgery my wife became a kidney donor for our friend Eileen, who had been in a decades-long struggle with kidney disease. She had begun to spiral down toward complete renal failure and needed either to start dialysis or receive a donated kidney. She was on the national waitlist for kidney recipients but knew that the list grows rapidly and outruns the supply of kidneys available from donors. As of February 2011, there were over 110,000 candidates for organ donations listed as on the United Network for Organ Sharing (UNOS) waitlist.[14] Of these, almost 90,000 are waiting for kidneys either from deceased or living donors.[15] Although placed on the waitlist, Eileen's prospects for receiving a kidney from a deceased donor were small in the short term. The median wait-time for receiving a kidney in Eileen's age group was four and a half years according to the 2003–4 statistics, with the wait trending upward over previous periods. Almost a year before Eileen approached acute renal failure, however, my wife began to consider the possibility of donating one of her kidneys to Eileen. Deb soon told Eileen and her husband about her intent, and they were rather taken aback by the offer. How do you respond when someone offers to give you one of their body parts? Over the following months Deb reiterated her desire, and come the following December, she received a call from Eileen that her kidneys had dipped below 5 percent capacity, and she soon needed to go on dialysis or have a kidney transplant. Just five months after my open-heart surgery we embarked on another surgical journey. One month later, Eileen had a new kidney and avoided dialysis altogether. Deb was left with a scar and one kidney.

Before the surgery both Eileen and Deb underwent an extensive battery of medical exams. Were they a match by blood type, tissue matching, and crossmatch? Was Eileen a truly eligible candidate for a transplant? Was Deb healthy enough to donate one of her kidneys? Did she have two kidneys? Ten percent of the population is born with only one — surprising but true. A CT scan revealed that she did indeed have two kidneys. Extensive exams revealed that Eileen and Deb were a match. In addition, the current generation of immune-suppressant drugs virtually guarantees that the host will not reject the donated kidney, if the levels of the anti-rejection medications are properly monitored. If Deb had not been a match for Eileen, however, her kidney could have been donated to another person who was a match while that person's living donor could offer their kidney to Eileen if they were a match. The Chicago hospital where Deb and Eileen's kidney operations were performed, Northwestern Memorial, has a current record of sixteen people, eight donors and eight recipients, who were crossed over to secure good matches for all recipients. This is kidney juggling at its best.

The exams revealed that Deb was very healthy and able to donate one of her kidneys. Contrary to all other forms of surgery, the living organ donor receives no physical benefit from the donation. While the risks of the surgery are managed and low, they do exist. She was warned that one possible outcome could be death, although statistically this occurs extremely rarely. We were surprised to discover that the life expectancy for kidney donors is *longer* than that of the general populace, mainly because the only ones allowed to become kidney donors are the healthiest people. And should a donor go into kidney failure for any reason, that person would be ushered to the top of the list of those waiting for an organ donation. But with these good statistics came the warnings as well, including a reminder that donating a kidney would constitute a "preexisting condition" should my wife need to change insurance companies. She could be denied coverage because of her good deed.* Assessing risk became part of the donation process.

Before the surgery, Deb canvassed our family to see if she had the support of our daughters, her sisters, and me. Our first concern was for her well-being, but our anxieties lessened as we realized the high probability of good outcomes for her as well as Eileen. We saw Deb's clarity about the donation. Her confidence in God and her conviction that this was the right thing to do for Eileen were powerfully persuasive. Deb's greatest need would be for good recovery time, and her workplace enthusiastically supported her donation and gave her the time needed for the operation and recovery. We also recognized that no one in the family was in any foreseeable danger of kidney failure. And we saw that Eileen's life could be lengthened, her quality of life improved, her need for dialysis eliminated, and she could continue to enjoy fruitful years of ministry in the Dominican Republic.

The most moving aspect of the kidney donation was the way Deb approached this act out of love and concern for a friend. She was willing to run a risk to offer something of herself so that someone she loved could live. We and everyone close to Deb watched in awe as this selfless act unfolded — and in this drama we saw the gospel enacted anew. We had heard this story before. Very familiar. Christ's selfless act of giving himself so that we could live sent out ripples through time and these moved Deb to care and give, even though it involved risk and pain for her. As a high priest, Jesus offered a sacrifice but in his case the priest did not offer the life of a sacrificial animal but himself (Heb. 7:27). He was the unblemished sacrifice who, through the Spirit, offered himself so that we could be reconciled to God and cleansed of our moral defilement (Heb. 9:14, 28). Christ's offering on the cross was proportionally and substantively

---

* The Affordable Care Act of 2010, which brought healthcare reform for all Americans, guarantees that all people with preexisting conditions can obtain health insurance.

more efficacious than Deb's donation of a kidney to Eileen. Yet the surgery bore within it the *imitatio Christi*. Christ did not need to die for himself, and Deb did not need to have a kidney removed. Both gave and underwent pain so that others could live. Christ's act cut a path for Deb to follow, and Deb's gift became a powerful message to us all about offering a living sacrifice for the benefit and the well-being of another. We are all inspired to good works by her deed.

The donated organ becomes a true gift of grace. Just before the surgery, one of the chaplains at Northwestern Memorial came in to talk and pray with Deb. This wise and experienced minister reminded Deb and all of us that the kidney was a gift, and as such it would become Eileen's kidney and not Deb's kidney in Eileen. When we give a gift, the giver offers it freely and joyfully. If it is a true gift there are no strings attached and no expectations of return. The gift becomes the property of the one who receives it. For Deb, this meant releasing her kidney, and the care of her kidney, completely to Eileen. For Eileen this meant that she had a new kidney that was fully under her care and totally for her benefit. This was a true gift of grace.

The ancient term "grace" (*charis*) was well-known in the Greek world as "that which produces joy (*chara*)." People used the word to describe the help and bounty that benefactors gave to their communities. Such gifts indeed produced joy. Grace, then, was not only a favorable disposition but embraced concrete acts that augmented the well-being of others. Such gifts are not purchased by the ones who receive them, but they do produce joy and thanksgiving (*eucharistia*). As Deb was wheeled off to the surgical suite, we saw an image of the fundamental lesson of the gospel — God's grace toward all humans through giving Christ Jesus for us and for our salvation (Eph. 2:8 – 10). And God's deed became a call to imitate that example. Buried within God's great acts of benefaction we discover God's summons to do as he did. And Deb showed us all how to do that.

Those who receive bioprosthetics and organ donations, whether from deceased or living donors, turn us back to the lessons of community. One of the strangest experiences for humans is having our life depend upon an organ that came from another human being or animal. How does a person live peacefully with a heart, lung, or kidney that came from another human who met a tragic end? And how can we conceive of being kept alive through a biological mechanism that was harvested from a nonhuman relative (to put this in Native American terms)? Both bioprosthetics and donated organs appear, at first, to bring us into an unnatural union with another of God's creatures. From the time we were cut off from our mother by the severing of the umbilical cord, we have become accustomed to regard ourselves as independent and on our own. We breathe on our own, our heart beats on its own, our kidneys process our blood on their own. But at the moment of transplant we become dependent upon another to sustain our most basic human functions. And surgery facilitates this union. But that bond formed by cutting and sewing dispels the myth isolation and total independence. In the end, we do depend deeply on our land and fellow creatures for food, our parents for nurture and direction, our social networks for labor and relationships, and God's creative hand and providence, which placed us in this matrix of life.

In the end, surgery joins the recipient with another and shows our connectedness and bonds in a way that is unparalleled beyond the womb. The dependency becomes an organic testimony to how we, as humans, are dependent upon others for our life in myriad ways. We are not on our own since God has created us to live together in dependent community. The transplant of an organ brings us all back to this most basic lesson of human existence. Paul acknowledges our dependency upon God saying, "We do not live to ourselves, and we do not die to ourselves. If we live, we live to the Lord. And if we die, we die to the Lord; so then, whether we live or die, we are the Lord's" (Rom. 14:7–8 author's translation). But we, as humans, are also called to each other's side by the one to whom we are bound. And his commandment is "that you love one another. Just as I have loved you, you also should love one another" (John 13:34; 15:12–13; Rom. 12:10, 16). The other-directedness of Jesus teaches us to be for the other (1 John 3:16). We are dependent upon God and others for all that pertains to life from the moment of conception to the time when we are laid in our grave. Between those two moments we walk together on a common road, eat our common food, breathe our common air. The road is filled with all our relatives and we need them, and they us, in this journey of life — "all our relations." Spare parts sewn in through surgery awaken us from our illusory dreams of independence.

5

SURGERY
AND JUSTICE

THE BILL FROM THE HOSPITAL AND MY PHYSICIANS FINALLY arrived. For the surgery and the hospital stay of twelve days, seven of those in ICU, the total came to just over $350,000. Needless to say, there were a few nervous moments as my wife and I wondered whether our insurance was going to pay the total cost. We saw no reason for it not to cover all the charges. Every procedure had been pre-authorized, and our family physician had submitted the proper referrals. Our HMO plan promised to take care of everything, save for a deductible from the hospital. When the claim form from the insurance company arrived, we were pleased to see that the charges were indeed paid and the bill from the hospital was only the $150 deductible. No way could we have paid the total cost of the surgery. To do so would have meant stepping into deep debt, a financial hole from which it would have taken an extremely long time to extract ourselves. We were grateful for the good insurance policy offered by my employer, Wheaton College, which was taken out with a reputable and well-established company.

In contrast, at the time my wife worked with the underserved in DuPage County, Illinois, a prosperous area that, in 2000, ranked number twenty-three among the one hundred counties having the highest median household income in the US.[16] In 2010 DuPage County held second place among the 102 counties in Illinois for overall health and is number one for health factors, that is, the health behaviors, clinical care, and the social, economic, and physical environments offered its residents.[17] Yet my wife's former employer, the largest healthcare agency in the nation offering medical services to the underserved, has a number of clinics in DuPage County.[18] Many refugees come through the clinics, along with those of low or no income who do not have insurance of any sort. They receive subsidized care through this agency, which serves as a safety net for the thousands of DuPage residents who never had or who have lost healthcare insurance. During the economic downturn that began in 2008, Deb witnessed an uptick in the number of patients who suddenly found themselves without any insurance coverage due to the loss of a job and their inability to find new employment with benefits. She, along with the doctors and physician's assistants in the clinics, were able to offer basic healthcare but often had to depend on the sheer goodwill of hospitals and specialists to take care of the more serious issues the patients might have. Surgery is a big-ticket and luxury item that is not automatically or readily available to all who walk into the clinics.

After my bill for open-heart surgery arrived, I often wondered what my options and outcomes would have been had I needed to rely upon the sometimes fragile net this social service organization offers. In the most prosperous nation in the world, millions of people cannot readily access the healthcare and surgery that is part of my employer's benefit package. In 2007, 47.5 million people in the United States had no health insurance with the 2010 count at closer to 50 million.[19] The chasm between the need and access to adequate healthcare is a breeding ground for illness, unwarranted suffering, and death. However it happens in the end, we need healthcare reform that will open the doors of access.

I wonder about justice, especially given the way two nations where my wife and I previously lived, Costa Rica and Great Britain. They both offer good and accessible healthcare to all their citizens. On a recent trip to Costa Rica, I heard both a car-rental agency employee and a retired professor from the University of Costa Rica celebrate the medical treatment they received from the "Caja" (the government agency that administers the national medical service). Unsurprisingly, questions of justice arise in the middle of the operating theater. Should adequate healthcare only be available to the economically privileged? Can the Christian citizen simply say, "I have mine; let them find theirs"?

The scenes in the gospel story where Jesus healed everyone (Matt. 14:36; Mark 6:56; Luke 6:19) are glimmers of the day when "'He will wipe every tear from their eyes. There will be no more death' or mourning or crying or pain, for the old order of things has passed away" (Rev. 21:4, which echoes Isa. 25:8). The universality of the promise offered by the gospel is one of the most astounding aspects of the Christian faith. Jews and Gentiles, women and men, the aged and the young, the strong and the weak, and "persons from every tribe and language and people and nation" (Rev. 5:9) are all invited to become partakers and participants. The inclusive embrace of the gospel is an offer of salvation for the soul as well as remedy for the body. The ill, lame, and blind were brought to Jesus who healed them all, even those who many regarded as excluded from the promises given to Israel due to their ethnicity (Matt. 8:5 – 13; 15:21 – 28). The Gospel is about inclusion through grace.

The unaddressed invitation and the unlimited access in these scenes, however, do not find their global counterpart in contemporary surgery and healthcare in general. On the day before my surgery, the *New York Times* reminded us that "The world's wealthiest two billion people get 75 percent of all the surgery done each year, while the poorest two billion get only 4 percent and often die or live in misery as a result."[20] Cataracts are left untreated, birth defects are not fixed, surgeons are not available, operating rooms are scarce. In Africa there is only one operating room for every hundred thousand people, while in Western Europe, North America, Australia, and New Zealand there are fifteen for the same population, twenty-five rooms per one hundred thousand in the most wealthy Asian countries. Surgical theaters in many of the poorest places lack the essentials, from instrument sterilizers to oxygen tanks. My surgery was distressingly costly and unavailable to others in the world who suffer in the way I did. While the signs of God's redemptive action were present in the operating theater on the day of my surgery, the sterile technologies and the well-practiced skills were also a sign that the least and the lowly are excluded. I presented my insurance card before entry. Not everyone has one.

My experience also stands in stark contrast to the discontent found in China's healthcare system. In some hospitals, police officers are needed to protect doctors from attack by patients and their relatives. In 2006, there were 5,500 attacks against Chinese medical workers. A *New York Times* article by Sharon LaFraniere reports stabbings and arson against doctors and even a riot of two thousand people that was organized after a three-year-old did not receive treatment because the family could not pay the equivalent of $82 in fees.[21] Dissatisfaction with medical treatment in China is high and vast numbers of poor do not have access to the care they need. A wide gap stands between healthcare spending by the government and the needs of the people, reports LaFraniere, bringing the medical crisis in the country to a boil.

Restricted access is even more dramatic in other countries. The lack of trained physicians and nurses, coupled with few opportunities for surgery and the lack of availability of basic medicines, have left many countries with growing numbers of crippled patients. Liberia is able to invest only $4.00 per year per person in healthcare, compared to $5274.00 in the United States. In other countries corruption undermines the medical systems as inferior and ineffective medications are sold on market. As the Dominican musician Juan Luis Guerra sings, "Y la medicina aquí no se cura" ("And the medicine here does not heal").[22]

While in the hospital, a patient-care technician from Nigeria told me about doctors in his country who would not treat patients with even the simplest procedure or medicine if they did not receive payment first.[23] Patients in Nigeria must often have relatives buy the medicines they need while in hospital, and then these are hidden under their pillows. Misdiagnosis was common and even shortened the life of the president of his country. The surgical facilities were far from adequate. He left Nigeria to find a better life for himself and his family and is now working in DuPage County alongside many international doctors and nurses from the Philippines, Russia, Latvia, and elsewhere. Such migrations have produced shortages of medical personnel in numerous countries around the Majority World. As Andrew Green, Professor of International Health Planning at the University of Leeds, remarks, "The world faces a profession-staffing crisis.... Rich health systems face similar pressures to poor countries in terms of recruitment and retention of staff. The difference lies in their ability to plunder, using enticing packages, the poorer health systems. The global labour market has led to a new form of neo-colonialism."[24]

Whether I wished to acknowledge it or not, issues of justice were present there in the operating theater, ICU, and the cardiac floor of my hospital. The type of surgery I had undergone, along with the prosthetic valve that saved my life, are out of reach for the majority of people in the world who need the same procedure. Millions in my own nation are in the same position. I will continue to enjoy many years of good life and joyful interactions, but their lives will be cut short. Is there any hope to remediate the dramatic global and national inequities in healthcare? Or should we simply be satisfied with the notion that healthcare, and its most specialized manifestation in surgery, are properly the domain of the rich and well-employed? Are they privileges, like the BMW with the high mileage guarantee and "free service" for the first 50,000 miles, or do healthcare and access to surgery rise to the level of being a basic human right? As long as we regard healthcare as a privilege of the privileged alone, we can and will do little or nothing toward making access to it more universal. The Affordable Care Act (ACA) of 2010 was a major national step toward assuring access to good healthcare for all — the poor, the rich, and those in the middle.

What can we do to make sure that the type of basic medicine my wife offered to the underserved and advanced care that I received in surgery is more accessible to people on the margins, both here and abroad? For one, technology can help bring the cost of surgery down in places where resources are scarce. Not many years ago, the cell phone was an item that few people had or could afford, regardless of their place on the globe. Now this technology has shrunk in size and cost and has become ubiquitous throughout the globe, even in rural villages of poor nations such as Bangladesh. Lowered prices have multiplied access to communication. The phenomenon is similar to the way television antennas jut from the roofs of squatters' houses in shanty towns scattered throughout the Majority World. Underscoring the accessibility of cell phones and televisions does not mean that these technological marvels have brought unmixed blessings since they may break traditional communication networks or import alien and unhealthy cultural influences. But they are models for how helpful medical technologies may become widely accessible. Multiplying access through larger and more streamlined production has lowered costs and brought elite market items to the poor. As technology develops, techniques for undertaking major surgical procedures will become cheaper and more accessible.

In their editorial discussion on "Prosthetic Heart Valves: Difficult to Make Something Simple," Didier Lapeyre and his colleagues observe that "Whereas large financial investments presently involved in transcatheter valve delivery [that is, heart valve replacement through a cardiac catheterization procedure], little recently has been done for the much larger population of younger patients and children world-wide who need a durable heart valve substitute that performs safely without warfarin anticoagulation."[25] "Catheter-based valve technology" may become part of the global answer to heart-valve disease. But the authors conclude, "We believe, however, that it is also important for industry to focus on development of improved devices for the great majority of patients needing valve replacement." The problem of heart disease runs throughout the globe and does not limit itself to those nations that have the available resources to counteract it. Can heart-valve surgery not only be perfected but made accessible to peoples everywhere, as have technologies such as the television and the cell phone?

For surgery to more fully resonate with God's work of restoration, surgeons and those who place technology in their skilled and artful hands must keep seeking to widen the door marked "Access." This could be an alternative name for the medical relief agency CURE International (cure.org), which began to treat children with hydrocephalus with a new procedure. Developed by CURE doctor Benjamin Warf, the procedure avoids the shunt-based system used for over sixty years in favor of a noninvasive and simpler treatment than used historically. Two thousand children come into the world with this condition in Uganda alone, but now there is hope for them via affordable and accessible technology.

Second, the rich countries of the world should attend to funding the training of nurses and doctors to meet the present and future needs in our own countries so that there are fewer openings in our hospitals and clinics for medical personnel from the Majority World. At the same time, immigration policy needs reform so that fulfilling our own medical needs is not the primary criteria for granting a green card. If we have shortages of medical personnel, we can address these through education and scholarships rather than pilfering the scant human resources found in countries of the Majority World.

Third, global collaboration by physicians, nurses, midwives, hospitals, and medical schools can help raise the standards of medical training and treatment in the Majority World. If a school or hospital in the West includes, as part of its mission, collaboration with institutions in the Majority World, we can raise the level of surgical care elsewhere while, at the same time, introducing present and future medical personnel here to the needs and issues facing the global medical community. Collaborative educational arrangements are already becoming a primary concern of colleges and universities in the United States. Such strategic alliances can become true "win-win" situations for all participants.

Fourth, medical personnel from the West can volunteer their time, from weeks to years of service, in seeking to shore-up medical care in other parts of the globe. Agencies such as CURE, the Christian Medical Association, the Luke Society, and Doctors Without Borders all make available such opportunities. Christians have been at the forefront of developing such organizations. While the focus of such foundations has been the needy in the Majority World, the poor within our own country often find themselves unable to access adequate surgical care. We must develop more charitable organizations like the Larry King Cardiac Foundation, whose mission is to "provide funding for lifesaving cardiac procedures for individuals who, due to limited means and no insurance, would be otherwise unable to receive lifesaving treatment."[26] The expansion of healthcare opportunities is a problem that government, business, and charitable organizations can solve together. Historically the church has been a leader in helping provide healthcare and needs to find its theological resources and will to fill that role once again. Such practical charity arose during the early centuries when the church was persecuted but it continued afterward through the founding of hospitals. Indeed, the church "established a role, previously unknown in the ancient world, of charitable concern for the sick, which ultimately led to the creation of both *diakoniai* [a diaconate that served the poor who were ill] and the earliest hospitals."[27]

Finally, medical care within our country should be available to all, as Jesus made available both bread and healing to those who came to him. Amidst the legitimate debates regarding the most effective means of delivering healthcare to those who need it, we should not allow Jesus' encompassing compassion to pass from view as we travel down the political road. He commended the Good Samaritan for taking the wounded man and attending to his needs (Luke 10:25 – 37). He saw the need and responded while others passed by, absorbed with their own occupation, interests, and fears. Jesus left no person hungry and offered medical care to the multitudes. We follow his example, bringing the *imitatio Christi* into healthcare. While we will not see a world where there are no more tears until Christ's return, that vision of the end informs our hopes and labor in the present. Before the Affordable Care Act, one out of every six people in the United States had to rely on no more than their income to pay for healthcare, and these people were from the lower to middle income brackets. Their access to healthcare was extremely limited. They could not pay for the type of surgery I needed in order to live. The future justice for all becomes the goal we seek in the present age, although we may not expect to obtain it fully and ideally. The alternative, however, is not to do nothing but to act according to the eternal values of the kingdom of God now, those exhibited daily in Jesus' ministry. We must strive to make the healing ministry of surgery available to all, if indeed we seek to become imitators of his example.

6

RECOVERING UNDER THE SCARS

EIGHT MONTHS HAVE NOW PASSED SINCE THE SURGERY. A COUPLE of months ago I finished ten weeks of cardiac rehab sessions with a group of ten other heart patients, mostly men, who had valve replacements, bypasses, heart attacks, and stents inserted to allow blood to flow freely through the arteries supplying their heart. Three times a week we shared stories in the locker room and then got down to the business of recovery. In every class we spent ten minutes on each piece of exercise equipment as cardiac nurses monitor our EKG tracings and pulse rates through the wireless telemetry attached to our chests. They circulated to check everyone's blood pressure, took us through warm-up exercises, monitored our exertion level, and then provided instruction on heart-healthy habits. Time to turn the iPod down and listen. We became experts on salt and stress, diet and exercise, heart anatomy and blood pressure. The outcomes were good, and we celebrated the "graduation" of class members every few weeks. The certificates always came with a word of encouragement to keep up with the healthy habits learned. I'm doing just that.

I walked away from each session feeling just a bit stronger and more hopeful. Recovery was in full swing. My wife and friends commented on my progress back to health, letting me know that I looked better and sounded stronger week by week. Hope blossomed a bit more with each rehab graduation I saw and every comment I received. Normal routines of life seemed less and less like mountains to scale. Stairs held little terror.

Surgery brought great pain and weakness, driving me lower than I have ever journeyed. But the recovery has been steady and sure, although I am always acutely aware of the scar that bisects my chest. My surgeon was patient enough to suture it using cosmetic techniques so I would not bear a "zipper" scar running up my chest. Two round scars below the suture line mark the places where he inserted the chest tubes. The wires binding my sternum together sometimes make me ache — signaling a change in the weather? The wires and the scars will remain as reminders of the destiny-altering event. Faithful application of Strivectin cream cannot erase the scars, though time will reduce their swelling and redness.

The recovery period has lasted longer than I anticipated. Somehow the statements the surgeon made about how long this would take did not sink in, and the word "rehabilitation" whizzed by unnoticed. Stories I hear about how long others took to recover make me believe, however, that I am progressing well. My surgeon and cardiologist confirm this assessment with every visit. Surgery tows behind it time for recovery that may be long or relatively short. This period between surgery and health calls for patient waiting, watching for signs of normalcy, taking blood tests, showing up for regular assessment by the physicians, listening to others' comments and advice. Though the operation lasted a short time, recovery just takes its own sweet time.

God designed healing and recovery to occur this way, a frustration in a world where instant is too slow. We must wait, patiently, with time ticking slowly as we long for a quick return to the rapid swirl and swing of life. Bones and incisions are in no rush to heal. We know that mended bone is stronger than bone that has never broken, so the slow process can bring good benefit. But the waiting time of recovery also becomes a Sabbath in our life, a reminder that in a world of good and fruitful labor there must be seasons for rest and renewal. We experience this daily as we sleep; our bodies and minds stressed by the day are renewed with each eight-hour hibernation. The Sabbath of God is made for humans and our good (Mark 2:27).[28] The rhythms of labor and rest were blueprinted by God when he built this world and all who live in it (Exod. 23:11 – 12). We follow his example (Gen. 2:2 – 3; Exod. 20:8 – 11). God is patient and has planted rest and slowness in the midst of our hectic hurry.

People who undergo surgery often come away from the event with a renewed resolve to slow things down, to take time for children and spouse and friends, and to enjoy life. Jack Crossland, our landlord in Scotland many years ago, repeatedly admonished me, "Slow down, young man, and smell the roses. Life is too short for all this rushing about." I was a twenty-something from Chicago, and these were dreadfully hard words to hear. But God says the same as we recover from surgery, reminding us that resting is as important as running. He renews his creation, us included, through slow processes that are well designed and effective. As businesses, schools, and even families or ourselves seek to compress two hours of labor into one, skip lunch and sleep to get the work done, rush frenetically from this to that, and consume the last day of rest each week in more giddy activity, our time to recover and renew becomes diminished. And our bodies become ill, our emotions sink, our relationships cool, and there is no time to pray. Surgery loudly summons us to return to rest in order to allow God's daily and weekly recovery to occur.

While God wondrously designed our bodies to recover from wounds, others participate in the process. They bring food, insist that the patient gets out of bed, assist as she or he takes the first weak steps, offer words of wisdom and encouragement, and carefully watch over and monitor the patient in this time between. After Jesus raised Jairus' daughter from the dead, the Lord instructed him and his wife "to give her something to eat" (Mark 5:43). At times surgery goes somewhat wrong and the surgeon must open the patient again to correct some unnoticed or newly developed bleeding. Jesus himself healed a blind man and then asked, "Do you see anything?" The

man responded, "I see people; they look like trees walking around."
Jesus then placed his hands on the man's eyes again and "his eyes
were opened, his sight was restored, and he saw everything clearly"
(Mark 8:23 – 25). Patients are dependent on others to arrange their
environment and orchestrate their care so that healing can occur.
The Samaritan was filled with pity upon seeing the person on the
road who had been robbed, stripped, and beaten. He bandaged the
man's wounds, poured in the ancient medicines of oil and wine,
transported the beaten man to the inn "and took care of him." After
a night of vigilant nursing, the Samaritan charged the innkeeper
saying, "Look after him ... and when I return, I will reimburse you
for any extra expense you may have" (Luke 10:29 – 37). The Samaritan serves as an example for all, but also models the conduct of
Christ. Recovery is a community event, not something left solely to
the patient.

There is a shift, however, that occurs during the recovery period.
The patient takes up more and more responsibility for their own
care. The dance between the patient and caregiver changes as roles in
the partnership change. The patient's first steps can be painful, ones
that they may be reluctant to take. These can be awkward moments
between patient and caregiver, with toes inelegantly stepped on as
the music changes and the dancers turn. The patient's goal is to take
the lead, and the caretaker's goal is to facilitate the transition. In the
middle of this dance, fears and anxiety easily arise about the patient's
ability, doubts about full recovery surface, and concerns about
relapse overshadow the sunny joys of survival. Balance is off. The
patient continues to need realistic words of hope even as strength
returns. The caregiver wisely exhorts the patient to stand up and
move but does so with compassion and understanding. The period
of crisis has passed but prayers and support are still needed.

The synergy between patient and caregiver, the weaker and the
stronger, echoes the mystery of God's dance with humanity. Human
responsibility does not deactivate God's agency in the world, and
God's providential care for humanity does not leave us or allow us to

be idle. God planted the garden in Eden and made the trees to grow food, but he placed Adam "in the Garden of Eden to work it and take care of it" (Gen. 2:8, 15). Healing after surgery has both a divine and a human dimension as does all life under God. We pray and act, trust in his care and exert ourselves, and hope for his provision while we calculate the cost and outcomes. The synergy defies full explanation: we work and labor while knowing that the resources for and fruit from our labor come from God alone.*

Even when the recovery is complete, the patient is left with scars that last through life. Some of these are hidden from public view, and others are so discrete and small that the patient will cease to notice them over time. But the scarring may be more dramatic and evident to everyone. Not all scars can be removed or minimized through plastic surgery. A woman may hide a full mastectomy through breast forms, bras, and clothing, but scarring on the face, hands, or arms are often in full public view. Unfortunately, people are not always accustomed to seeing others with scars. They stare and quickly turn their heads, but the scarred person notices. The scarring can be a source of embarrassment or shame. The physical pain from surgery subsides as the social pain begins, a new cutting that may produce emotional scars. But even scars out of sight can remain as painful reminders of the disease or injury that the surgery sought to correct, testaments that the patient's life has been altered in irreversible ways. Life will go on, but there has been a change. The story of our ailment and our surgery is always with us, told not just with our lips but with our scars.

Despite the anesthesia and the medications that dull the pain, surgery is surrounded by suffering. Our body has a condition that is abnormal, threatening, and festering, and it may produce agony, fear, and uncertainty. Surgery is a saving and redemptive intervention, but it carries risks and sometimes unexpected outcomes. The intent

---

*Speaking of the ministry to the Corinthians, Paul said, "I planted, Apollos watered, but God gave the growth" (1 Cor. 3:6 author's translation).

is to heal, but suffering accompanies the process. Before my surgery I had become symptomatic. Short of breath and weakened, I could not do what I had done for years. I could not cycle, continue my summer schedule of research and writing, nor travel to teach overseas. Plans suddenly stopped short, and it was frightening. The arc of my life was being bent in unexpected and uncontrollable ways. The saving surgery then brought pain that, while managed with medications, still throbbed underneath. While I was grateful that my condition was diagnosed quickly and that the operation spared me from diminished physical ability and even death, surgery still hurt. It also left me less robust and sent new thoughts about mortality charging into my life. The horizon moved, overnight it seemed, bringing an acute awareness that death's street address isn't that far away. Life is grand, and I celebrate God's gift with great joy. Facing its end, however, brought deep sorrow. Surgery advances at our weakest moment when abnormality and mortality march boldly onto our field. Scars are the battle wounds left from the skirmish.

Why is there so much pain? It may appear in news reports dispatched from far away, or it may come into our neighborhood. When it arrives at our house or in our lives, it catches us by surprise and sends deep shudders down our spine. It touches both body and soul, showing itself in red wounds and red eyes. In this short book I cannot work through the whole question of *why* we suffer and endure pain in this life.[29] Pain has taken up residence through all God's creation, which is filled with decay and groaning. But that is not the end of the story since God's full and final redemption is coming (Rom. 8:18 – 25). I've learned over the years, and now through surgery, that the gospel of Christ lays out before us the best resources to help us face and frame our pain and scars. There is both pain and promise in the gospel.

We joyfully celebrate God's "Good News" every Christmas when we remember the babe's birth in Bethlehem. But suffering marks the beginning of this story. At a tender age, Jesus was quickly swept away to Egypt when Herod the Great sought to kill him (Matt. 2:13 – 18).

And we read in the gospel (Matt. 27) and remember in the Apostle's Creed that, after years of proclaiming the kingdom of God, he "suffered under Pontius Pilate, was crucified, dead, and buried." He identifies with us when he was scourged and crucified, entering into our pain and suffering, and taking on the penalty for our sin (2 Cor. 5:21). He was truly "a man of suffering, and familiar with pain" (Isa. 53:3). There was physical suffering and deep emotional pain as Jesus hung on the cross and cried in agony, "My God, my God, why have you forsaken me?" (Matt. 27:46). Suffering is at the very heart of Christianity. The frilly versions of our faith that have no place for suffering miss the gritty, tearful, agonizing, and confused heart of the gospel. It's all about suffering and glory, not just glory alone (1 Pet. 1:10 – 12). We will indeed share in his glory, but also his sufferings (Rom. 8:17). As George MacDonald said, "The Son of God suffered unto death, not that men might not suffer, but that their sufferings might be like His."[30] We come to him with our deepest pain and sobbing, knowing that he knows, knowing that he is with us. He too has scars.

I took Communion at church before the surgery, in the hospital, and again when I was able to return to Sunday morning services. There was bread and the wine, offered with the reminder, "Broken for you; shed for you" (see 1 Cor. 11:23 – 26; Matt. 26:26 – 29). The whole gospel story is present in the bread and wine. As we take them, we remember the cross (1 Cor. 11:23 – 25; Matt. 26:26 – 28) and anticipate his coming (1 Cor. 11:26; Matt. 26:29). These are signs of Christ's salvation through his death, resurrection, and coming again. Remembering is not simply about recall but participation with him. God's grace is there at that moment and we share in it. But it is grace bought through his brokenness and pain. He knows our pain, and we understand his. I found amazing comfort in the middle of my fears as I took communion in those occasions around my surgery. I saw Jesus' death and life in a fresh way and was reminded of what he went through so that I could have life and hope. Now the surgical scars in my body are also marks of suffering and salvation, despair and hope. They are signs that point back and point forward, and point to Jesus. They remind me not only of what I have gone through but what Christ endured for me and everyone else.

The operation becomes a chapter in our life's story. We start to mark events from before or after the surgery, remembering years and months in relation to this most critical moment. The scars stand as monuments to that story, which is now integrated into our lives and part of who we are. We may turn bitter and angry because we needed an operation that left a scar, or we may rejoice knowing that we have been spared through the operating table. In either case, the scars do not go away, although we may interpret them in different ways. They remain as markers and signs of the story that is now part of our identity.

The image of Jesus after the resurrection is that of a person who was identified not by clothing, haircut, or even eye color. After he rose from the dead, he showed his disciples his hands, feet, and side, all of which remained scarred. This was the Lord who called them, taught them, and did miracles. But he was also the crucified Jesus, the one who suffered when nailed to the cross and was pierced after he died. When he appeared to the disciples on the first day of the week, he said, "Peace be with you!" After that "he showed them his hands and his side." At that moment "the disciples were overjoyed" (John 20:19–20). These were the marks that identified who he was, something even doubting Thomas understood: "Unless I see the nail marks in his hands and put my finger where the nails were, and put my hand into his side, I will not believe" (John 20:25). Though he had been raised from the dead and his body had been transformed[31] he still bore the marks of his crucifixion. We know him today as "Christ crucified" (1 Cor. 1:23) even though he overcame death. Our resurrected and risen Lord is

This Byzantine cross has five marks representing the pierced hands, feet, and side of Jesus' body.

the crucified one who carries scars. These are marks of pain, sacrifice, and redemption.

But there is a problem here, as St. Augustine recognized in his book *The City of God*.[32] How can God raise a person so that their identity is maintained while, at the same time, he recasts the person so that they are restored to beauty? If someone's story includes surgical amputation, will the person's identity be lost or changed if the amputated body part is restored? The problem is especially acute for Augustine as he considers the wounds still present in Jesus' body after the resurrection. He discusses the special case of martyrs for the faith whose wounds are beautiful marks of their devotion to Christ. Their wounds will remain, but not those of the rest. "While, therefore," he says, "no blemishes which the body has sustained will be present in the world to come, we are nonetheless not to deem these marks of virtue blemishes, or call them such" (22.19.1150). Augustine is in line with Paul. The resurrected body will be glorious and transformed. The hope of the kingdom of God is that the lame will again walk and the blind will see (Isa. 35:1 – 6; Matt. 11:2 – 6), with lost limbs restored. The Great Surgeon's work will be complete and perfect. But as the body repaired through surgery preserves signs of pain and restoration, we may expect that the resurrected body will still carry signs of the scars that tell a person's story. Is this only for martyrs, as Augustine says, or for all of God's people who have seen him work in the midst of pain? Are the only beautiful scars those of Christians who have lost their life for Christ? Or are our surgical scars likewise reminders of the cross of Christ? Bodily resurrection will restore us to full functionality, the goal of the Surgeon, but this does not mean the complete elimination of faded scars. They tell our story.

The apostle Paul identified the wounds from his sufferings as "the marks of Jesus branded on my body" (Gal. 6:17 NRSV). He understood his wounds and sufferings for the gospel as signs of his identification with Christ. These "marks" or *stigmata* are not the mystical wounds that some have seen on the bodies of particularly devout Christians in church history such as Francis of Assisi or Julian of Norwich. Their *stigmata* were said to appear on hands, feet, or the back as signs of identification with Christ. The word itself in Greek, *stigma* in the singular, simply means a mark or a brand. Medical literature sometimes refers to surgical wounds as *stigmata*, the signs or marks left by the surgical procedure. To be sure, these are not the same as either the *stigmata* Paul speaks about or those that some in church history have seen. But the scars of surgery are indeed marks and signs that remind us of the greatest sacrifice for good, the cross of Christ. He was wounded on the cross for our salvation, and he bore the scars of his crucifixion after the resurrection. As suggested previously, surgery is a medical act that inflicts a wound to bring good and healing, and as such it echoes God's means of redemption through the cross. Suffering and salvation meet here. The scars of surgery remain through our life to testify that good can come from the bowels of pain. They are signs that point us back to Jesus, the one crucified and risen.

My life changed dramatically that July when my surgeon cut me open on the operating table. The event brought great trauma and altered my physiology. I am still the same person as before, but I'm also different. The operation bisected my life into two periods: "Before Surgery" and "After Surgery." I am pleased to have a scar greet me every morning and remind me that my life, though changed, was spared by the surgeon's knife. It is my scar, my life, my story.

7

THE WORST THING HAPPENED

THIS LAST WEEKEND I WENT TO VISIT MY LONGTIME FRIEND Earle who had just undergone surgery to replace his shoulder. He was talking and alert the day after surgery, and his wife, Ginny, told me of her surprise that Earle would be able to return home the next day. She was a bit overwhelmed by the prospect of caring for Earle at home, but Bonnie, their eldest daughter, was there to help.

The surgery was a success, just as everyone had prayed and the doctors had expected. Earle was the proud owner of his own titanium prosthetic shoulder, a true bionic man. He had a blue shoulder harness, which pumped cool water around the surgical site to assure that the swelling would be kept at a minimum. Earle looked a bit like a gladiator who had been knocked down but would soon rise up to stand another day. The room was filled with smiles and chatter, hope fulfilled and fears allayed. It was a good day after surgery. Before long he would be behind the wheel of his car and perhaps chop wood again near his cabin in the North Woods.

But in the course of our conversation, Ginny and Earle recounted the tale of a woman they knew well who had received a kidney donated by her daughter. My ears perked like a Doberman's, fixed to the sound and cadences of this surgical story so similar to the one Deb and Eileen had experienced together eight months previously. Eileen had been doing well with her new kidney and was back serving people in the Dominican Republic. Deb had returned to work and showed no ill effects from having donated a kidney. But the story Earle and Ginny told had a different ending. The kidney that the woman had received from her daughter had failed. She was now on dialysis. And her daughter was experiencing terrible guilt, they recounted, since she had done everything she could to help her mother who was in renal failure — but her gift failed, and now she could do no more. Her good act did not bring relief. The cost of the surgery was not reflected in the bills from hospital and physicians but calculated in this mother's and daughter's bodies and hearts. Hopes were crushed, fears returned, the future clouded over with dark and low storm clouds.

Surgical patients, their families, their friends, and the medical staff know together that things can and do go dreadfully wrong. Surgeons and their colleagues expend their best efforts to follow standard protocols to help ensure minimal risk and favorable outcomes for each surgery. Specialists are put on the case as needed. Hospital staff check blood type, take X-rays, and prepare the operating suite according to rigid sterile protocols. Members of the surgical team explain the procedure to the patient and answer any questions. Both the surgical team and the patient scrub to avoid any infection. The team assembles with the patient in the surgical suite but before proceeding calls a "time out" to verify all the data regarding the patient and procedure type. The anesthesiologist puts the patient under, then signals to the surgeon that the procedure may begin. Everyone performs their coordinated steps with utmost care to keep the patient from harm and to avoid malpractice. Yet there is a crash cart nearby and any other equipment or supplies needed should things go wrong. Extra units of blood are on hand. Before surgery, the patient or their parent or guardian signs a waver after reviewing the risks. The physician and hospital administrator know that things can go wrong even with the best preparation possible: "Have you read the risks? Sign here." The life-blood of surgery is hope, but hopes can be dashed and replaced by despair. Things can and do go wrong, and sometimes they cannot be put right. The worst thing sometimes happens.

Risk cannot be banished from the surgical suite or the recovery room. A surgical procedure is an act of authority on destiny, but as in any contest there are always factors that can turn what seemed to be a winning ticket into a torn and dropped defeat. Even the shortest odds do not always end with a ride to the victory circle. Defeat in this race, however, may mean shortened life, persistent pain, permanent medical problems, or even death. Everyone knows that the stakes in this match-up are extremely high, yet hope drives surgeon and patient forward. We do not undertake surgery in hope of a bad outcome but rather approach it with careful planning, firm resolve, high expectation, and prayer. But a terrible thing can happen, and sometimes does. Sometimes the best is not good enough.

How can we cope in such times? Confusion descends, questions arise. Was this the right procedure? Were the right people involved? Did they proceed with care? Is this the right place? Should we have acted sooner? And, God, how did this happen? Why did it happen? What are we going to do now that it happened? Where *were* you? Where *are* you? Lost hope leaves a scarred and cratered landscape. The dissonant notes that led to the decision to operate remain unresolved as they clang together in cacophonous crescendo.

Loss is part of the human story and, indeed, of all creation: banishment from the Garden, death dealt to our First Parents and all created life, society divided and alienated from God. There is a weight and groaning before our many losses that cuts deep into the heart of human existence and of everything that lives. We are made to live, thrive, and survive, and we run with every ounce of our strength from harm and death. Even the ant and fly flee when chased and threatened. The longing for life and wholeness and the avoidance of pain and death is sown into the genetic code of every living creature. As humans we understand the processes and can take radical action against destruction and death, even to the point of being willing to face harm so that good may come. The surgical knife, we know, can heal, so we submit to its wounds in hope of finding relief from and resolve for the dissonance of disease. But the defeat of such radical hope can bring despair that cuts as deep and dark as the grave. We groan with all creation when the worst thing happens. We resonate with all our relations in death.

Paul wrote his letter to the Roman church with a deep understanding of the "bondage to decay" that is at the heart of all creation. Through the fall, "the creation was subjected to frustration, not by its own choice, but by the will of the one who subjected it" (Rom. 8:18–21). The author of Ecclesiastes, whom Paul echoes here, understood the futility of life in the face of death: "Perfectly pointless, says the Teacher, perfectly pointless. Everything is pointless" (Eccl. 1:2 CEB). When the worst happens in surgery, we are brought face-to-face with the question of the futility of our efforts and even of life itself. What can be done against that decay and death that hold to each creature tenaciously, allowing us victories in the skirmishes while knowing they will win the war? What's the point of the effort? What's the use? Surgery too seems "perfectly pointless" along with everything else.

But somehow, as humans, we refuse to live at that place of pointlessness and despair. We have children, we plan for tomorrow, we communicate and labor together, and each day we wake and fill our lungs and fix our breakfast and pour our coffee. It smells so good. We love and embrace, widen our circle and bring others in, and walk through the woods and fields just to enjoy life. We refuse to live at the point of futility and despair. We were dealt death and defeat, but God has sown hope so deep within our hearts that each day we walk defiantly and hopefully along the path of life.

Paul knows this hope. He almost shrugs off the despair of defeat and death as he says, "I consider that our present sufferings are not worth comparing with the glory that will be revealed in us" (Rom. 8:18). He lives in a hope that transcends death and leads on to the glory of God's final redemption for all creation, for all our relations. That hope is not just within the apostle's heart but is the stuffing of our existence, the juice and joy that gives way to all life at the present time: "For the creation waits in eager expectation for the children of God to be revealed," since in the end, "the creation itself will be liberated from its bondage to decay and brought into the freedom and glory of the children of God" (Rom. 8:19 – 21). Yes, he notes, there is "groaning" throughout all creation — and in ourselves. He watches and listens to it but understands it as the pain that will give way to birth, not ultimate death: "We know that the whole creation has been groaning as in the pains of childbirth right up to the present time. Not only so, but we ourselves, who have the first fruits of the Spirit, groan inwardly as we wait eagerly for our adoption to sonship, the redemption of our bodies" (Rom. 8:22 – 23). Paul teaches us that defeat and death do not present the final argument in this case. The closing and decisive argument comes from God who, through the resurrection of Christ, brings life and hope as the final verdict: "the redemption of our bodies." Things have gone terribly wrong, the worst has happened to humanity and all creation. But God brings redemption to humanity and creation through Christ's resurrection from the dead (1 Cor. 15 and 1 Thess. 4:13 – 18). We may grieve now, but not like those who have no hope.

The message of hope in the New Testament comes wrapped in tears. No Pollyanna and no "Glad Game" appear in its pages since the apostles embrace the pain and grief in life while allowing hope to prevail. Paul knows the Thessalonians grieved over the ones who died but calls them to grieve with hope and to console one another (1 Thess. 4:13 – 18). Peter is a human realist who knew both the joy of hope and the true grief of pain (1 Pet. 1:6). When the early Christians faced the death of the first martyr, "Some pious men buried Stephen and deeply grieved over him," even though he had been received by the exalted Son of Man (Acts 7:54 – 8:2 CEB). The lament was part of Jewish life (Lam. 1 – 5) and the New Testament authors understood such sorrow as well. We sit with others in their grief and confusion, questions and disillusion, all waiting for that unseen hope (Rom. 8:25).

The center of the gospel is the death of Jesus Christ, our Lord, who knew that his mission entailed suffering and death (Matt. 16:21; 17:22; 20:17 – 19; 26:1 – 2). Yet as he hung nailed wrists and feet to the beams of the cross, he cried out in a loud voice, "My God, my God, why have you forsaken me?" (Matt. 27:45 – 46). Creation itself joined in the lament since "From noon until three in the afternoon darkness came over all the land." Jesus evoked the words of Psalm 22:1 where David cried out in the confusion of lament, "Why are you so far from saving me, so far from my cries of anguish?" To him it seemed that God did not hear: "My God, I cry out by day, but you do not answer, by night, but I find no rest" (Ps. 22:2). The heart of the gospel beats with questions and protest borne out of despair. Yet Jesus' life ends without anger and accusation against God but with a confidence that shattered his confusion and defeat: "Father, into your hands I commit my spirit" — and with that he breathed his last (Luke 23:46). Questions and confidence are not enemies but they come together in the cross of Christ. Loss and defeat do not mean that God does not hear or that he cannot act.

The longing and love for life fills our breast with agony when things go wrong. Jesus in the Gethsemane garden said to those with him, "My soul is overwhelmed with sorrow to the point of death. Stay here and keep watch with me" (Matt. 26:38). When things come apart we look for the way out and look to God to rescue us: "My Father, if it is possible, may this cup be taken from me" (Matt. 26:39). While only Jesus died for the sins of the world, we enter into his suffering and despair when the worst thing happens. Any understanding of the gospel that does not embrace suffering, pain, disillusionment, and death is no gospel at all. Yet the gospel does not end with a final breath but with the studied confidence that can only come as all values and concerns are placed in the hands of God. The radical hope of the gospel is that though darkness overwhelms us on this Friday, God receives us and Sunday is coming. He has not forsaken us. He is the substance of hope.

In the midst of Jesus' suffering, he looked for help from others.

In the Garden of Gethsemane, he led the disciples into the place of despair and confusion, saying to them, "Sit here while I go over there and pray," then took his closest disciples, Peter, James, and John, along with him (Matt. 26:36 – 37). These three, however, could not stay awake with him (26:40, 43, 45 – 46). When arrested, "the disciples deserted him and fled" (26:56) and while he was on trial, Peter denied knowing him (26:69 – 75). Women who followed him watched from a distance when he died (27:55 – 56), along with "all those who knew him" (Luke 23:49).

The distance between Jesus and his followers at the time of his greatest suffering presents a confusing picture. We know they should have stood with him, risked their own safety to support him, offered their prayers as he sought the Father. The absence of others in the time of lament is crushing, and we know it is wrong. When Paul reached the end of his life, he stood trial before the Emperor Nero — alone: "At my first defense, no one came to my support, but everyone deserted me." He was not bitter, but indeed wounded, as he wrote, "May it not be held against them." But he was supported by the Lord who "stood at my side and gave me strength.... To him be glory forever and ever. Amen" (2 Tim. 4:16 – 18). Luke, his beloved physician, was there at the very end, however (4:11). We know why Luke was so loved. He was present.

When the worst happens, the greatest human need is for the presence of others who gather around the bed to hold the hand, to offer a glass of ice water, to just be present. The ones who come to occupy space with their distracted text messaging and web surfing or who come to talk all about themselves and their shopping expeditions are not the ones who are present. Rather, the people who stand in prayerful silence, in attendance, sensitive to needs, and responding with kind words and a warm touch are the people we want present. They do not need to have the answers, and they should not think that they have to resolve the dissonance of life and loss with a few hollow words. There are true words of comfort and hope that can be healing: "Therefore console one another with these words" (1 Thess.

4:13 – 18, author's translation). Friends and family of the one who has had the worst happen are called to the side to comfort as God does with those who are in pain and confusion. Indeed, Paul knows God as "the Father of compassion and the God of all comfort, who comforts us in all our troubles, so that we can comfort those in any trouble with the comfort we ourselves receive from God" (2 Cor. 1:3 – 4). The person who comes and sits and consoles another joins with God as they together surround the one who has had the worst happen to them. And the person who has lost knows they are not alone, never alone, not to the end of the age.

My surgery had a happy ending, and so did Earle's. He is recovering nicely and I am now back teaching classes, playing my bagpipes, bounding up the stairs, and riding my bike. But all surgical sagas do not end this way. The stories are as varied as the circumstances and the people who walk through them. Yet in this battle between life and death, hope and despair, we are not alone. God is with us, and others as well. The journey between the fall of creation and the final recreation is one we take together. Never alone. Never left. Never forsaken.

8

A THEOLOGY
OF SURGERY

WHILE I SIT IN WONDER AT THE RESTORATION AND RENEWAL
surgery has given me, I am also aware of living in an altered
state. The scar I see in the morning's mirror faithfully reminds me
of that. Having Brother Pig's valve in my heart, which I can feel and
even hear at times, is a surreal experience. Someday it may fail and
need to be replaced.

The surgery has restored me, but I still live with mortality and
imperfection. I do not despair but simply recognize that such is
the course of our life: strong and weak, endless possibilities and an
abrupt end, renewal and decay. This does not make surgery useless
but places it as a symbol of God's saving hand in the world, which
points us to the final day of restoration. Paul spoke of the day when
he "will transform our lowly bodies so that they will be like his glorious body" (Phil. 3:21). I have caught a glimmer of that event in this
surgery, and it makes me long for the dawning of the day. The scar
calls me to consider anew the cross and resurrection of Christ as well
as my own redemption.

Surgery is a medical procedure that gathers together the best of
human wisdom, experience, technology, and patience. Yet it is a procedure that evokes the great issues of human life. I did not expect
surgery to be a journey into the deepest spiritual experience of my
decades of life as a Christian. God did a wide work in my mind and

heart. It was not just about physiology but theology. Deep life with God in the middle of deep pain. The encounter with the surgeon, physicians, nurses, and other medical staff turned out to be a sweet time with the Lord himself, as he brought me on the journey of a lifetime. Many have said that they would never want to return to the most painful moments of their life, but they would not trade those times for anything. An odd truth that we cannot understand apart from the cross of Christ. Pain and hope, confusion and commitment, loss and restoration all join hands together. At this point we encounter the deepest wonder: that good can come where only pain seems to be present. We cannot understand this unless we look to Jesus, the one who hung on the cross and whom God raised from the dead.

Surgery brings with it lessons for life with God, theological lessons. The event does not stand separate and aloof from God's design for the world and humanity, nor is it undertaken in isolation from his providence. God set in motion a plan for the world when he formed it, the animal world and humanity, and he continues to carry out that plan through all successive generations. Surgery, the most invasive medical act, is part of that plan; it recognizes that something is wrong with the human condition that needs correction. The fall of humanity and this world are evident in the need for such a dangerous and dramatic intervention. Yet at the same time, surgeons carry out their technological art in the theater of hope, engaging in work that anticipates the final day of Christ's return when God will raise the dead and wipe away every tear from our eyes. Surgery may not be successful, and may not provide a perfect or enduring solution to a severe medical condition. It prefigures the final restoration of humanity, but it does not move the final moment of redemption out of God's hands or fully into the present. At best, it is anticipatory and, as such, a sign that signals hope.

Surgery brings us close to the way that God has chosen to work out human redemption. God intervened in human history by sending his Son into the world (John 1:14; 3:16) to become one with us in our humanity. He took upon himself the penalty for our sin as he hung upon the cross and, through deep, painful, and deadly wounds, he obtained redemption and life for all who call upon his name and seek his service. The violent intervention of surgery echoes the story of the cross since out of harm comes good, out of wounds comes life.

The surgeon stands alongside Christ, imitating his way and skill, by following his ministry of healing those who come with diseased bodies. The surgeon reaches out with technical skill and compassion to better the life of the one who lies on the table. But this medical practitioner works in company with others who are essential participants in the symphony of life. The patient is the recipient of the surgical intervention that includes a myriad of others in the operating theater, the recovery room, the hospital floor, or rehabilitation. Surgery is an intensely social event that echoes God's design for the human community. They work together for positive outcomes, each contributing to the well-being of a single person who has been brought low and now needs surgical intervention.

The operating room is a place where technology and biology come together, the one demonstrating humanity's great skill and innovation and the other calling us to look at God's intelligent design. Prosthetics are a prime example of the way God endows humans with endless creativity and art, yet at the same time they point to the gap between what we can fashion and what God has created. Prosthetics are a sign of hope and, at the same time, a call for humility. We can imitate God, but we cannot play God.

The greatest wonder in the surgical theater is the transplant, which involves the sacrifice one human makes for the benefit of another. The proclamation of the gospel is eloquent in that act of love and selfless giving. Some transplants involve the loss of one life. Yet here, more than anywhere, we see the connection we have as humans with others, even beyond the grave. There are deep mysteries here about death and life, and glimmers of the resurrection.

Surgery, however, is sadly limited to a select group of people who are able to access this level of care. Far from being universally available, the richest among humanity have access to the greatest surgical skills and services. A healthcare system that imitates Jesus, however, would allow open and full access to all who need such care. Jesus' healing ministry, we remember, was extended to everyone, including those on the margins. He did not limit his healing to the wealthy or even to those who held a special place among his own people. Surgery brings with it the deepest questions of justice and compassion.

We enter into surgery with great hope for a good outcome. Yet surgery entails risk. Sometimes the worst thing happens. Things can and do go wrong despite the best efforts of surgeon, medical staff, patients, and their supporters. Defeat and victory are the two ends of this playing field, yet despite the risk our deepest longing for life moves us forward. Surgery may bring us no relief but instead transport us into the heart of despair. In such cases, we lament together, as one, looking beyond defeat to God, into whose hands we are commended from our first to last breath. He is the Lord who gives life to the dead, and we console each other with these words.

I am not sure what tomorrow will bring. The bioprosthetic valve that keeps me alive has a limited service life. It may calcify and become as inefficient as my native valve. Reoperation is a real possibility some years ahead. But I am ready for that, knowing that I will not take that step alone. Surgery brings with it fears and pain, yet also hope and restoration. As Christians we live between the times, knowing that Jesus brought in the Kingdom of God through his life, ministry, death, and resurrection (Mark 1:14–15; Luke 17:21). But he also taught us to pray, "Your kingdom come, your will be done, on earth as it is in heaven" (Matt. 6:10). Surgery reminds us that we can taste the fruits of God's kingdom now and at the same time look forward to the final banquet that we will eat together with him when his kingdom fully comes (Luke 22:16, 18). The bright hope of morning sun shines into every operating room.

ACKNOWLEDGMENTS

ANY READER OF THIS BOOK WILL RECOGNIZE THE DEBT I OWE TO a multitude of people. Without them this book, and my life, would not be possible. Some are acknowledged here, although there are extremely important players whose names I do not know. All were significant players in the production of this book, and I am deeply grateful to them.

First of all, many thanks to my frontline medical team: Drs. James Carroll, George Kuzycz, Mark Nelson, and Physician's Assistant Robin Fortman. Your combination of skill, carefulness, and compassion have meant life to me. I also want to thank the medical staff at Central DuPage Hospital in Winfield, Illinois, for their excellent professional care in the operating room, ICU, and the Cardiac Unit. The other support staff at CDH fed me, kept my room clean, and helped assure that I would be infection free. Many thanks to them for doing their job well.

My family — they were right there by me. My brother, Charles, came — he always shows when needed. I've seen that throughout my life. My daughters, Gillian and Christiana, came and attended me, as did Penelope, my granddaughter. Their love and care sustained me. Christiana and my son-in-law, Josh, kept vigil in the hospital for many hours, many days, as would have Gillian had work not called her back to New York. I am deeply grateful for you all. My wife, Deborah, carried me. She was in the hospital day in, day out, night in, night out. Upon returning home she watched over me like a vigilant hen with a chick. Love is deep — I've seen it in her. No expression of thanks can match her constant care.

I also owe a debt of gratitude to our church, Gary United Methodist. We were new at Gary when I underwent surgery, not even members. But the church pulled out the stops to care for me and my wife. They visited, they prayed, they brought food, and were there for us. A special thanks to Rev. Tracy Malone and Patsy Sorrell for their pastoral care and to the women who knitted and prayed over the shawl given me. "Covered in prayer."

Finally, I would like to acknowledge the good support of my institution, Wheaton College. The school gave me the time needed to recover well before returning to the classroom. My colleagues visited and prayed, and they even read drafts of this manuscript. I'm honored to be part of this caring Christian community.

And in the end, all glory goes to God. He gives us life, sustains life, renews life, and gives us the hope of life. Thanks to you, Father.

NOTES

1. See Mark Noll's book *The Civil War as a Theological Crisis* (Chapel Hill, N.C.: University of North Carolina Press, 2006).

2. This is a principle concern of the member institutions of the Council for Christian Colleges and Universities. See, for example, the many papers on the subject on their website, www.cccu.org (accessed September 16, 2010).

3. René Leriche, "La chirurgie était un acte d'autorité de l'homme sur le destin," *Philosophie de la Chirurgie* (Paris: Flammarion, 1951), 163.

4. See the provisions of the FMLA at www.dol.gov/whd/fmla (accessed January 29, 2011).

5. See J. A. Kulik and H. I. Mahler, "Social support and recovery from surgery," *Health Psychology* 8 (1989): 221 – 38; Kathleen B. King, et al., "Social Support and Long-Term Recovery from Coronary Artery Surgery: Effect on Patients and Spouses," *Health Psychology* 93 (12): 56 – 63.

6. See S. Silberman, et al., "Aortic Valve Replacement: Choice between Mechanical Valves and Bioprostheses," *Journal of Cardiac Surgery* 23 (2008): 299 – 306; M. W. van Geldorp, et al., "Patient Outcome after Aortic Valve Replacement with Mechanical or Biological Prosthesis: Weighing Lifetime Anticoagulant-Related Event Risk against Reoperation Risk," *The Journal of Thoracic and Cardiovascular Surgery* 137 (2009): 881 – 86.

7. Homer, *The Odyssey* 10.208 – 425.

8. Mark notes that the drink was a mixture of wine and myrrh, a concoction believed to ease suffering (Pliny, *Natural History* 14.15, 92 – 93). The gall Matthew mentions was a bitter substance, perhaps given as a sedative (Babylonian Talmud *Sanhedrin* 43a).

9. Many of us have read Upton Sinclair's *The Jungle* (New York: Simon & Schuster, 2004, originally published in 1906) and Eric Schlosser's *Fast Food Nation: The Dark Side of the All-American Meal* (New York: Houghton Mifflin, 2001), both of which have been made into movies (1914 and 2006).

10. See Nicolette Hahn Niman, *Righteous Porkchop: Finding a Life and Good Food Beyond Factory Farms* (New York: HarperCollins, 2010).

11. Richard Twiss, *One Church, Many Tribes: Following Jesus the Way God Made You* (Ventura, Calif.: Regal, 2000), 96. See also Randy S. Woodley, *Shalom and the Community of Creation: An Indigenous Vision* (Grand Rapids, Mich.: Eerdmans, 2012).

12. Twiss, *One Church, Many Tribes*, 97.

13. Winona LaDuke of the Mississippi Band of the Anishinaabeg describes the Native American understanding of the relationship between humans and other creatures. They are our relations, "our brothers, sisters, uncles, and grandpas. Our relations to each other, our prayers whispered across generations to our relatives, are what bind our cultures together. The protection, teachings, and gifts of our relatives have for generations preserved our families. These relations are honored in ceremony, song, story, and life that keep relations close — to buffalo, sturgeon, salmon, turtles, bears, wolves, and panthers. These are our older relatives — the ones who came before and taught us how to live." Winona LaDuke, *All Our Relations: Native Struggles for Land and Life* (Cambridge, Mass.: South End Press/Minneapolis: Honor the Earth, 1999), 2.

14. See www.unos.org (accessed February 19, 2011). UNOS manages the organ-transplant system in the United States.

15. Current data regarding national patient waitlists can be found at the Organ Procurement and Transplantation Network (OPTN) website: optn.trans plant.hrsa.gov (accessed February 19, 2011).

16. "List of Highest-Income Counties in the United States," *Wikipedia*: en.wikipedia.org/wiki/Highest-income_counties_in_the_United_States (accessed May 6, 2014).

17. "Illinois 2010," *County Health Rankings and Roadmaps*: www.county healthrankings.org/illinois/overall-rankings (accessed May 6, 2014).

18. *Access Community Health Network*: www.accesscommunityhealth.net (accessed May 6, 2014).

19. "America's Uninsured Crisis: Consequences for Health and Healthcare," *Institute of Medicine of the National Academies*: http://iom.edu/Reports/2009/ Americas-Uninsured-Crisis-Consequences-for-Health-and-Health-Care (accessed May 6, 2014) and the Kaiser Family Foundation, http://www.kff.org/ uninsured/upload/7806-03.pdf (accessed November 5, 2010).

20. Donald G. McNeil Jr., "Surgery: Poorest 2 Billion Remain in Dire Need of Fully Functioning Operating Rooms," *New York Times* (July 13, 2010): D6.

21. Sharon LaFraniere, "Discontent on Health Care Spurs Violence at Hospitals in China," *New York Times* (August 12, 2010): 1A.

22. Juan Luis Guerra, "El Costo de la Vida" *Areito* (RCA International) music CD.

23. A personal report, July 23, 2010.

24. Andrew Green, "Nursing and Midwifery: Millennium Development Goals and the Global Human Resource Crisis," *International Nursing Review* 53 (2006): 14.

25. Didier Lapeyre, et al., "Prosthetic Heart Valves: Difficult to Make Something Simple," *Journal of Thoracic and Cardiovascular Surgery* 139 (2010): 1373.

26. *The Larry King Cardiac Foundation*, http://larrykingcardiacfoundation.org/ (accessed May 6, 2014).

27. Gary Ferngren, *Medicine and Health Care in Early Christianity* (Baltimore: Johns Hopkins University Press, 2009), 138.

28. "The Sabbath was made for humankind, not humankind for the Sabbath" (NRSV).

29. Some good resources to help us work through the topic are C. S. Lewis, *The Problem of Pain* (New York: HarperOne, 1996); D. A. Carson, *How Long, O Lord? Reflections on Suffering and Evil* (Grand Rapids, Mich.: Baker Academic, 2006); Christopher J. H. Wright, *The God I Don't Understand: Reflections on Tough Questions of Faith* (Grand Rapids, Mich.: Zondervan, 2008).

30. George MacDonald, *Unspoken Sermons, First Series*, quoted in Lewis, *Problem of Pain*, vii.

31. See Paul's discussion about the resurrected body in 1 Corinthians 15.

32. I am indebted here to the good discussion in the book by my colleague Beth Felker Jones, *Marks of His Wounds: Gender Politics and Bodily Resurrection* (Oxford: Oxford University Press, 2007), 28 – 29.